GOD, COURAGE, AND COVID

GOD, COURAGE, AND COVID

A THOMISTIC APPROACH
TO THE COVID-19 PANDEMIC

NICHOLAS JONAS

The Slattery Center for the Ignatian Humanities
Student Fellow 2022-23
Faculty Mentor: Dr. Patrick Clark
The University of Scranton

.

"Even though I walk through the darkest valley, I fear no evil, for you are with me; your rod and your staff, they comfort me."

Psalm 23:4

CONTENTS

ACKNOWLEDGMENTS

The very notions of this project are a blur in my memory. Other than that, I had been seeking a different challenge, one that lives far outside of my comfort zone, that I will either grow tremendously intellectually or struggle under pressure. I am proud that the former has been the superior outcome of this project. Naturally, I keep my nose down in the sciences, dabbling with classes within my major, Biochemistry Cellular & Molecular Biology. I have only recently developed this interest in philosophy and theology because of the great exposure many of my mentors have allowed me. I respect and acknowledge that philosophy is the fundamental process of living in this life oriented towards the truth. In contrast, theology is living this life guided by the Holy Spirit towards the good so that we may partake in the next with our Heavenly Father. This realization is nothing less than a blessing, having the support of so many and understanding why one should bother with this critical thinking of being and reality.

With all this being said, I'd like to begin by thanking Dr. Patrick Clark, who mentored me throughout this project. We began by discussing the project, transitioning from ideas about exploring Thomistic theology to a more "applied" project pertaining to Thomistic principles to one's ability to flourish during the pandemic. Dr. Clark helped me find sources, taught me what a passive voice was, and critiqued my writing, furthering my ability to grow. We explored various ideas and theologians/philosophers together, and I am proud of our final project here.

I would also like to thank Dr. Sarah Kenehan for her guidance and support, along with the Slattery Center for Ignatian Humanities at the University of Scranton. Dr. Kenehan and Dr. Clark coached me on the project and encouraged me to always dig further. One of the great aspects of the Slattery Center was the requirement for presenting your project, in which I found holes in my argumentation to better my ideas. I also met with many other students, both in my fellowship and outside, fostering a great sense of community.

Drs. Chris Fremaux and Duane Armitage were also a huge help, opening my eyes to Kantian philosophy and postmodernism. From this, I have developed a genuine drive to know more about this realm of philosophy and, eventually, explore Kantian thought, postmodernism, and Catholicism. I first had Dr. Armitage in my freshman year, for intro philosophy and then for ethics in my sophomore year. Through his mentorship, I soon began talking to Dr. Fremaux and found myself in his mentorship. Both have afforded me great intellectual gifts; I am grateful for this.

Besides these professors, I'd like to recognize and thank Brian Kenny, who has been a mentor for me and a good friend for numerous years. It is kind of fascinating that we both have a passion for philosophy, despite our work in the sciences. Brian attended Notre Dame, where he studied both engineering and philosophy, and when I was applying to colleges and even during my freshman year, he encouraged me to investigate philosophy and learn to think like a human. I am glad I listened, and as Brian says, I, too, think God may have put me in the wrong century. Besides this, Brian has been a great friend and a great person to take advice from, and the lessons he has shared with me are priceless, including his handicap on the golf course.

Fr. Richard Ricard, who is also cited in this project, was also an immense help. Fr. Rick is the pastor of my home church, St. Bernard in Rockville, Connecticut, and he often discusses the nature of the love of God, and the Holy Spirit, with me, which solidified my understanding for both my personal sake and this project. In addition, I gained a lot from his homilies and cited his Christmas Homily of 2022 in this project since it spoke to me about the trust in God we must take in order to flourish. The way Fr. Rick delivers his homilies is unlike any other priest I have ever celebrated Mass with, and I would like to thank Fr. Rick for his support and inspiration.

Writing a book during the academic year, for an undergraduate, was much more difficult than I could have ever imagined. Between tests for my academic courses plus the research and writing for this project, I was stressed, needless to say. Whenever anything got too much, some of my best friends would tell me to take a break, and we would leave campus. Andrew, one of my best friends, would always find a way to turn anything I was freaking out about into something I could manage. Blaring music together and getting lost in the sticks of Pennsylvania was incredibly fun, and funny enough, we ended up at my friend Gary's house somehow. Gary and his family were always welcoming and encouraging. My roommate Ethan would always make sure I was handling everything well and would always make sure that I was still remembering that he would always support me with whatever I needed. Nate took time out of his day to help me practice presentations and would always give great feedback, in addition to offering their support for me and my project. One of my best friends from home, Mark, would always call me when I was away at school to see when I was coming home so we could either plan a day at the slopes snowboarding, or go hiking, which kept me motivated. I am truly blessed to have these friends and to share this project with them in its completed state.

Finally, I'd like to thank my mom Stella and my sister Samantha for their continued support and their genuine interest in what I have been doing with my project. Sam would always call me at school, and we would take turns sharing college stories and asking each other for advice, both of us supported by our mom. Mom would always be there for us and supporting us in any way she could. This dedication she had for us is what I highlight in her, the ability to put her two kids first before herself. Without any of the aforementioned people, this project would not be possible.

Introduction

COVID-19's profound effect on life led many to question their faith, questioning the nature of a God that would allow for the suffering and pain felt worldwide. On the other hand, numerous individuals reported a greater or more profound faith during the pandemic, wherein one study found that in fourteen countries surveyed, 10 percent of people reported a stronger faith, and only 3 percent reported a deteriorated faith.[1] In a separate study, both religious and nonreligious individuals were surveyed regarding anxiety during the pandemic, finding that the stressors of the pandemic strengthened both ideologies further, meaning Christians reported a stronger faith, whereas the nonreligious reported even deeper skepticism towards religion altogether.[2] The implications of these

---

[1] Pew Research, "More Americans Than People in Other Advanced Economies Say COVID-19 Has Strengthened Religious Faith" (2021).
[2] Francesco Rigoli, "The Link Between COVID-19, Anxiety, and Religious

studies and the relationship between religion (particularly Christianity and Catholicism) and COVID-19 are further investigated here to highlight elements of faith during COVID-19 and what effect theistic belief or lack thereof has. Specifically, the element of theistic courage, defined as the courage informed by the Holy Spirit, demands consideration to establish how such courage may be exemplified best and inform action during the pandemic. This discussion serves to explore why faith enables individuals to cope with the stresses of pandemics, exploring the nature of theistic courage and how it can drive an individual's ability to flourish in a pandemic in accordance with God and reason. Namely, the manner in which the individual perseveres with the unique limitations and restrictions of the pandemic will be discussed, as well as how the individual may articulate decisions in accord with reason regarding her health and the call to love as Christ did simultaneously.

The first focal point of this discussion emphasizes arguments surrounding truth and objectivity to better accentuate the objective nature of reality and how this objective nature points to God as its fundamental source. The discussion here follows that the universe has objective attributes, including beauty and the call to morality, where the source for objectivity and universal truth must be God, further explored via the objective goodness defined in the following ontotheological discussions. A discussion on the nature of God follows, engaging in philosophical and theological discourse concerning God, facilitating key emphases of established truth and objectivity. This section also further investigates the individual's innate desire and yearning toward God, driven by the broken human condition. To contrast this, a depiction of reality without God will be discussed, namely from a Nietzschean perspective, and the purpose of this discussion aims to highlight why God must be by examining the Nietzschean account of reality, which is defined by the will to power and a lack of objective morality and value. This comparison then emphasizes the fundamental nature of morality and allows for a clearer evaluation of what reality may resemble, with this lack of the objective good. The objective nature of morality then calls for the highest and most perfect good, and as Aquinas will argue, God remains the highest good because the human being is called to an objective morality, and this must be true, considering the objective nature of the good thereby demonstrating God as source, following Nietzsche's characterization of a godless reality. This stark contrast allows for a clear view of the nature of God, and the role of God in the flourishment towards the good, where the driving unknown in this discussion is the unique relationship between God, this role in flourishing, and the COVID-19 pandemic.

The next portion of this discussion begins with an examination of virtue, followed by a discussion of courage and structural differences between habituated and infused, or theistic, courage. Before any discussion of courage may begin, the nature of virtue is discussed, which provides a foundation for arguments surrounding the informing of courage, whether theistic or not. This discussion on virtue emphasizes how the virtues inform each other and allow for the proper flourishing of the self towards God. The structure of Aristotelean virtue is discussed, namely, to serve as a foundation for the discussions surrounding informed virtue.

While the primary emphasis is placed upon courage, what follows also explains why *authentic* courage demands prudence and justice for one's informed evaluations and actions aimed at the good. In the context of COVID-19, courage is called for in numerous instances, including vaccination policy, education strategy, and the courage to flourish during such a time. The virtue of courage consists in a mean between risk and certainty, which requires finding a median between these two limits, where this balancing between "extremes" applies to all the virtues, but the manner in which it applies to challenging situations such as the COVID-19 pandemic are discussed, wherein the regulation of one's behavior may sustain her pursuit of the good amidst difficulty. Although it may appear that hope or the ability to flourish is lost during a pandemic, I argue that maintaining this authentic courage and a relationship with God is what allows for one's ability to flourish.

CHAPTER ONE

Objective Reality

Before a proper discussion on theistic courage may occur, it is essential to begin with a discussion of the reality in which we find ourselves. This reality has certain characteristics that are definitive in nature, which then give rise to certain calls of the self, driven by a force beyond the self. In other words, we can define this reality as existing separately from, or above, the desires of the self, which order the self to act according to what is objectively true, an objective truth. Some contemporary philosophy notes objective reality as governed by cultural norms or beliefs, yet the fundamental nature of these accounts appears to be identical to a great extent, noting that the call of morality governs the ability of one to flourish towards the good. The foundations of objective reality are discussed in this section, with emphasis placed on the collective features of reality and the role of God in an objective nature.

Evidence of an Objective Nature

The nature of reality entails an objective framework, evident in "the good," morality, and the intricate order of the universe itself. The emphasis here is placed upon the yearning for truth and the good, as described by Immanuel Kant,[3] since Kant argues humans experience a breathtaking sense of awe arising from questioning the universe and nature, as well as value and morality.[4] This vastness and the unknown drive a sense of vulnerability, of not knowing where observed objective truth emanates from, or the universe itself for that matter, which in turn gives rise to a longing for truth. This demonstration of vulnerability arising from the human condition and its innate questioning of reality serves as the basis of an account of the objectivity of truth and the good.

---

[3] 1724-1804
[4] Matthew Levering, *Proofs of God* (Baker Publishing Group: Baker Academic, 2016), 12.

Aristotle notes that the highest good is happiness, following the logic that morality is objective when this pursuit of the good is in accord with reason.[5] In other words, in pursuing the good, happiness is regarded as the end, where rationality in accord with reason acts as the guide to this end. This follows the argument that morality is objective since the call to the good is universal, and pursuing the good follows the same pattern, wherein following the objective good is to live in accord with the call of the soul.[6] Aquinas argues that this call of the good is indicative of an objective being that orders reality.[7] The pursued good serves as the final end of what is desired most; however, one cannot pursue the good in opposition to objective truth since truth serves as a guide to the good, and following Aquinas's argument, God. The objective nature of truth and the good, therefore, serves to emphasize God as the foundation of reality and the source of morality, meaning that the pursuit of both goodness and truth leads to God.

If excellence or goodness were not objective, then morality would be a subjective interpretation, yet the

[5] Aristotle, Martin Otswald, *Nicomachean Ethics* (Prentice Hall, 1962), Book 1, §7.
[6] Aristotle, Otswald, *Nicomachean Ethics*, 14-19.
[7] Levering, *Proofs of God*, 68.

nature of reality dictates that there is a universal call for compliance to morality, such that when followed, one finds the good. Since the nature of the traits of flourishing is objective, one therefore cannot conform them to one's own wants or desires. Following the Thomistic approach to the soul and its orientation towards God, the desires of the soul are aimed at God as their final end, and therefore, these desires stem from an objective source. When the objective nature of reality and the call to morality is established, the individual finds herself oriented toward a final state of goodness, happiness, and love, characterized by Aristotle as *eudaimonia*. This initial orientation sheds light on what is most good, illuminating virtuous behaviors that promote flourishing. Ultimately, the highest forms of these rest in God, the source of the objectivity of morality. Therefore, when the good is pursued in accordance with goodness and love as guiding principles, the individual finds herself arriving at the highest forms of happiness and truth within God. Because morality is objective, it is independent of the wants of societal and personal desires, meaning that the objective good will remain as is and not change because of human desires. Since God is the source of morality and truth, and since the call to the good is objectively true, we can rest upon the fact that God creates the rational being intending to love and do good.[8] This call to truth is objective in nature, driven by God creating us with the sole purpose of loving in accord with reason, given free will.

Goodness, therefore, cannot be based on individual preferences since truth from God informs actions because they are ordered toward a transcendent good. If good were subjective, there would be no unified call of the good, with ultimately no objective good. The nature of the good is objective and is clear in how we respond to suffering and challenges. Following that God is the objective good, we can conclude that truth is objective, like a fabric determined by the human condition to know, that holds humanity together and calls us all to the good and love.

Responding to the good is an innate response to our condition;[9] one responds to the call of morality without requiring much reflection on helping, loving, or wronging others. On the other hand, anti-ethical responses are deemed so if an action fails in its intent to act toward the good or if the individual fails to

---

[8] John Cottingham, *Why Believe?,* (Continuum: Continuum International Publishing Group, 2009), 39.
[9] Ibid. 19.

recognize the good and aims her intent elsewhere, including the possibility of evil. The human condition then calls for a rational and proper perception regarding the demands of the good and shapes our experience of reality. The reality disclosed in one's unique experience suggests the good as a unifying factor amongst people, and Aquinas concludes that being must coincide with the pursuit of the good.[10]

Truth and goodness are impartial necessities that govern reality, in which truth and goodness are mutually implicative and dependent. Their objective nature is established in everyday life, in acts of compassion or love for others, particularly when society faces a pandemic with an overwhelming number of unknowns. In short, the objective nature of reality is dependent upon such a God, in which God is regarded as both its structure and source.[11] The next point of discussion surrounds discourse around the existence of God, following the objective nature of reality indicative of God. However, this argument can be furthered by deliberating on classical theological and philosophical reflection and employing this in the depiction of the good and morality assumed here. The Platonic model,

---

[10] Cottingham, *Why Believe?,* 25.
[11] Ibid. 29.

which serves as the foundation for Aristotelean thought encompassing the good, argues that *eudaimonia* is found through philosophical inquiry. For Plato, happiness is the ability to pursue the philosophical life, which consists of meditation and meaningful aforementioned philosophical inquiry.[12] Further, Aristotle and Aquinas depart similar thinking regarding the contemplation of the highest good, where Aquinas's view is within reach of the majority, yet Aristotle contends only those with the ability to fully actualize the philosophical life may achieve this vision of the highest good. For Aquinas, beatitude then becomes an act of grace from God, even for those without the capacity for philosophical reflection, where, again, Aristotle argues that those with this ability to comprehend philosophical thought, namely the educated or wealthy, may arrive at this vision. Realization of this ability, however, necessitates the agent be disposed to the moral virtues over her lifetime and engage in consequential practice so that she may aim her being and vision at the good.[13]

---

[12] Patrick Clark, *Perfection in Death* (The Catholic University of America, 2015), 108.

[13] Clark, *Perfection in Death*, 109.

The Will

Aquinas then departs from the established perspective of the natural, or the acquired, virtues, in which Aristotle associates virtue with patterns of habituation of the will aimed at the good. In this difference of thought, Aquinas contends that the divine assistance offered through the infused virtues grants for perfection beyond human capacity.[14] Considering the fragility of the human condition, Aquinas then distinguishes the natural end of flourishing from the higher supernatural end of beatitude, which cannot be achieved through human capacity alone since this end is transcendental in nature, exceeding human ability. An external influence aids the agent in being guided towards this supernatural end, namely sanctifying grace, which bestows the infused virtues of faith, hope, and love (*caritas*), as well as the gifts of the Holy Spirit.[15]

Since the human good includes not just physical well-being, Aquinas contends that a threat to the physical state of well-being is not substantial enough to

---

[14] Rebecca Konydyk De Young. "Power made Perfect in Weakness: Aquinas's Transformation of the Virtue of Courage," *Medevial Philosophy and Theology* 11, no. 2 (2003): 174.
[15] Angela McKay, *The Infused and Acquired Virtues in Aquinas' Moral Philosophy* (University of Notre Dame, 2004), 14.

withdraw the agent from pursuing the good; there must be something else averting her act.[16] At a fundamental level, this obstacle dissuades her from acting; she may not pursue the good to the extent the martyr would, but this does not mean she lacks virtue or does not recognize the good whatsoever. In this case, Aquinas will then recognize courage in a different facet, wherein if one lacks the strength or ability to dismiss a threat without compromising the good, she may ward off the threat by "courageous aggression,"[17] which enables the agent to contest the threat. If this fails, she may engage in "courageous endurance,"[18] which enables her to evade or resist as best she can.[19] Clearly, Aquinas's model differs substantially from the Aristotelean insofar as the individual who aims at the good and encounters difficulty yet overcomes this while exemplifying courage, or at the bare minimum, does not engage in behavior that detracts from the good. Courage, therefore, becomes much more accessible in the Thomistic approach. Establishing the love for God when exhibited in an act of courage can be exemplified

---

[16] Konyndyk De Young, "Power made Perfect in Weakness," 154.

[17] Rebecca Konyndyk De Young, "Courage as a Christian Virtue," *Journal of Spiritual Formation and Soul Care* 6, no. 2 (2013): 306.

[18] Konyndyk De Young. "Courage as a Christian Virtue," 306.

[19] Ibid. 306.

by the individual who follows Christ's example. One may argue that the Thomistic approach becomes less accessible since courage cannot be formed through deliberate effort, which is true if one does not look to Divine Grace as source. Besides the love exemplified by rational beings, Aquinas then argues that nonrational beings are also driven by a steady state of love, in which beings of a community seek a common good to flourish together.[20] Here the rationale lies in the sense of care for others, also seen in the animal world in which animals seek a common good for their groups by aiding in survival and aiding each other in evasion of threats. The significant difference here lies in the state of the intellect, in which the rational animal operates in accord with reason purposefully aimed at the good and has the ability for the divine influence of the will, something that distinguishes the rational animal from the nonrational animal. Here, this allows for the rational animal to be directed by the good.

A Godless Reality

Following this discussion on God and the good, it is appropriate to explore a scenario in which there is no

---

[20] Clark, "Perfection in Death," 191.

God, wherein this discussion emphasizes human experience and its relationship with reality as a whole. Friedrich Nietzsche[21] most notably argues that "God is dead" and maintains that the individual's natural inclination is not to follow the objective good since there is no objective morality in his argument.[22] Because there is no objective morality for Nietzsche, he argues that the will to power is the mechanism of value and that any form of "morality"[23] is driven by willpower.[24] The logic behind this view follows that the will to truth and knowledge is merely the guise for the will to power, meaning that anything aimed at the good is aimed at one's ability to further one's power or status in the world.[25] Nietzsche therefore concludes that truth cannot be objective, following that an endeavor of "truth" for Nietzsche is not possible, but rather the true means of success for Nietzsche relies upon a survival of the fittest approach.[26] The pursuit of truth, then, is aligned with a power struggle. This path to power calls upon biological

---

[21] 1844-1900

[22] Cottingham, *Why Believe?,* 41.

[23] There is no morality for Nietzsche, however in this hypothetical scenario where there is only the will to power, what we know to be morality would be purely constructed of the will to power rather than pursuing the good

[24] Duane Armitage, *Heidegger and the Death of God* (Springer International Publishing, 2017), 94.

[25] Ibid. 12.

[26] Armitage, *Heidegger and the Death of God*, 13.

instincts, a Darwinian approach, to fight for superiority and gain ground on others to survive, and in this lies Nietzsche's approach to the mechanism of reality.

Because he maintains there is no objective meaning to reality, Nietzsche is an atheist by instinct, advocating the rejection of the Platonic premise of truth and love being one, the ultimate good. For Nietzsche, objective reality is a guise for the will to power, a rejection of Platonism in its entirety, as truth and love must be discarded. When this lack of objective good becomes accepted, there is no possibility of an ultimate source of objective truth.[27] Subsequently, if there is no God, then there is no objective morality nor any objective purpose or meaning of existence other than the will to power.

Nietzsche emphasizes that Western society evolved out of the Christian call to attend to the weak and therefore makes Western society an outright denial of the natural will to power.[28] The fundamental problem for Nietzsche with this denial of the will to power lies in its frustration with the inherent Darwinian instincts of survival, wherein the strong, by natural instinct, aim to further their own survival and produce capable offspring, thus preventing a weak society.[29] This is a

---

[27] Ibid. 45.
[28] Duane Armitage, *Philosophy's violent sacred* (Michigan: Michigan State University Press, 2021), 19.

12

reversal of Christian morality, wherein the vulnerable and victimized of society are supported by the strong out of love, when in fact, the natural order calls for the demise of the vulnerable in order to allow for the "survival of the fittest." Nietzschean philosophy applied to the COVID-19 pandemic would welcome the death of the infected and ill, as the resources spent on the dying could be better used elsewhere. This approach is unrealistic only because we are governed by the call to the good, namely morality, which orients the will towards love. Amid a pandemic, Christian morality calls for loving others, with particular care and attention given to the most vulnerable and neediest.

This presentation of Nietzschean philosophy shows what a Godless reality may look like according to one of the most prominent postmodernists, which for the sake of this paper means "the overcoming of metaphysics and ontotheology."[30] Because God is dead and there is no objective morality or goodness in the Nietzschean approach, it is then up to the individual to devise their own perceptions of reality and to derive their own morality or meaning. In doing this, Nietzsche argues that one's actions are governed exclusively by the will to

---

[29] Ibid. 23.
[30] Armitage, *Philosophy's Violent Sacred*, ix.

power, thereby enabling the strong to persevere and encouraging the weak to die off. Yet most people today would consider it abhorrent to reason that compassion should not be practiced, that love is a virtue of the weak, or that the call of goodness and love is merely a matter of subjective taste. If these were not objectively true, then one must discard the idea that reality cannot be informed by truth, yet there cannot be an absence of objective truth which governs reality. The weight of Nietzschean hermeneutics rests upon and gives definition to subjective truth and reality; the questions Nietzsche raises call for careful consideration, but even this brief account reveals that if compassion and love are recognized as core virtues of reason, then the reality of God must be objective.

The overall nature of objective reality can therefore be condensed into a few simplistic principles governed by the universal call to morality. This call to morality is evident in the innate desires of the individual in accord with reason, driven by love. This love, stemming from the love of God, enables the individual to pursue the highest good found in God, the source of this reality. The will of the individual is then oriented with the highest good and enables her to love as called for by the laws of morality. On the other hand,

Nietzsche approaches this question by deliberating on the means of the individual and why she may pursue the objective good. This approach then looks to the will to power as the subconscious mechanism for the actuality of the being and her pursuit of so-called truth, better described as just a means of being, since for Nietzsche, there is no truth. I present this here as a means to outline the fundamental nature of reality and the functionality of God in this reality, to better serve as a basis for the subsequent discussions.

CHAPTER TWO

Theological Implications and Proofs of God

The question of God's existence takes on even greater urgency during the COVID-19 pandemic, making it logical to examine the essential truth of such a God and arguments for God's actuality. Theologians and philosophers who demonstrate the existence of God are examined subsequently, as well as those who repudiate the demonstrability of God's existence on account of perceived flaws in the foundations of metaphysics. These sources will serve as the focal point for the paper's discourse on God.

Damascene

The arguments of John of Damascus (Damascene) focus on the necessity of a cause of reality and the inability of anything to come into being spontaneously on its own. Damascene's arguments consist of three demonstrations, the foremost being that "all things are either created or uncreated."[31] This suggests that any object or being can be in one of two possible conditions, existing or not. Following the principle that an object, other than the uncreated source, God in this case, can rest in its created or uncreated state, Damascene argues the object or being that exists may be altered through "…generation and corruption, or with respect to quantity, quality, or place."[32] Damascene argues the object or being that exists may be altered through "…generation and corruption, or with respect to quantity, quality, or place."[33] But regression to infinity cannot be since infinity is a concept of incessant expansion, lacking a beginning and an end; an infinite number of changeable things implies there would be no beginning, and so no beginning to the process of

---

[31] Levering, *Proofs of God*, 46.
[32] Ibid. 47.
[33] Ibid. 47.

change. If the entity responsible for all changeable things was itself changeable, then it could not be the entity responsible for all changeable things since there would have to be some prior entity responsible for it. And so, if there were no such thing as an unchangeable entity, there could be no entity responsible for changeable things in the first place; therefore, nothing changeable could exist.

It has been established that there must be a fundamental cause responsible for all changeable things that do not change since it is the source of everything that can change. Like Damascene, Aquinas follows the principle of the "unmoved mover," in which there may only be two possible conditions: an infinite number of moved movers or a singular unmoved mover that initiates all movement.[34] Akin to Damascene's supposition, Aquinas concludes there cannot be an infinite number of unmoved movers, and so some unmoved mover must possess a self-containing quality that allows the entity to set itself into motion and, by doing so, sets everything else subsequently into motion. In short, there can be no motion without a first unmoved mover since objects cannot put themselves into existence.

---

[34] Levering, *Proofs of God*, 62.

Damascene's second demonstration examines the highly ordered nature of the universe.[35] Perhaps the universe came to be spontaneously, but this argument fails to consider the highly ordered preservation of the universe observed in the perfect order of reality. If, by theoretical chance, the universe arose spontaneously, it would most likely perish as quickly as it came into existence; if its creation were spontaneous without order, this lack of order would fail to sustain it properly.[36] Scientifically, the chance of a habitable universe is infinitesimally small, impossible for Aquinas since there must be a clearly defined cause, and the maintenance of such an ordered universe furthers this improbability, not incorporating the likelihood of existing as intelligent forms of life into this supposition.[37] The solution to this, according to Damascene, must be that there is a divine order to reality and the universe. Therefore, Damascene concludes there must be an almighty Creator at play bringing being into reality.

---

[35] Ibid. 47.
[36] Ibid.
[37] Philip Goff, "Our Improbable Existence Is No Evidence for a Multiverse," *Scientific American* (2021).

Pascal

This reasoning continued centuries later, in which Blaise Pascal[38] presented arguments that center on the idea that one cannot attain complete happiness through anything bound by Earth, so something beyond the world must orient the will towards the good. Once the individual comprehends this structure of happiness because it is beyond herself and any physical domain, that she cannot attain happiness in anything within this life, she can then be directed to a source for happiness beyond this life, which resides beyond human ability and reason. Pascal argues that only when one faces one's own ineradicable unhappiness can they find God, and in Him, true happiness. The rational being has a natural inclination to the good and ultimate happiness, and when one follows this inclination to the end, they arrive at God. Similarly, when one attempts to supersede this intrinsic call to happiness and fill it with something other than happiness in God, one finds herself desolate and so must seek distraction, namely pleasure or lesser forms of happiness. The fundamental principle of orienting oneself to true happiness lies not in one's intellectual acuity but in one's commitment to the

[38] 1623-1662

integrity of the innate appeal to complete happiness. Pascal reminds us that "it is the heart that feels God, not reason: that is what faith is. God felt by the heart, not by reason."[39] A fundamental distinction is made here, namely that the heart is directed towards the love of God, and not a human comprehension of Him, which would be flawed, idolatrous, and incomplete. Because love is universally true and the love of God is the highest good, the individual must gravitate towards the ultimate object of her love rather than the concepts of such objects produced by human intellect.

Montaigne

Montaigne[40] spent much of his efforts criticizing Christianity and those who call themselves Christians, yet his work is just as instrumental to the theological process as Nietzsche is to philosophical explorations. Montaigne argues, "When once certain articles of their religion have been called in question and placed in the scales, they will soon be ready to throw into a like uncertainty all the other articles of their faith,

---

[39] Levering, *Proofs of God,* 111.
[40] 1533-1592

which had no more authority or foundation in their eyes than those which already shattered."[41] This specifically is Montaigne's response to how many French Catholics' faith wavered when Martin Luther spoke out against Catholicism. Because of this, Montaigne's take on Christianity is that Christians practice and call themselves Christians for the name and fear of death.

Montaigne's argument presented in this quote is fully and completely true; it is perfectly reasonable to question faith, especially during a challenging time, like during the reformation or a pandemic. Fear inoculates anxiety, anger, and frustration, and we exhibit these feelings partially by questioning the highest form of our beliefs. Montaigne's point is not wrong, as oftentimes we are Christians, not by reason of faith or love of God. Rather, Christianity comes from one's family, the fears of death, or the challenges of life. Because we are rational beings with tendencies for knowledge and trust based on physically observable phenomena, Montaigne's argument that people readily renounce and surrender their faith during high stress then makes sense, driven by the fragility of the human condition. The individual may not be as capable as she may think. For instance, high stress, and when placing this on God does not

---

[41] Ibid. 88.

fulfill our human desires of God, we abandon our faith and try to fill that void with something else. When he was close to death, Montaigne requested his last rites be given to him[42]. This final point supports what he argued that Christian's faith waivers. Ultimately however, it appears that Montaigne too was lost from God much like the Christian individual he describes. The significance here is that we call upon God when we are most vulnerable, yet I maintain that maintaining of this unique relationship is key to life, in which any number of challenges or obstacles can easily dissuade an individual from the highest good.

When Montaigne's predictions about the Christians become true, then what? Once one turns away from God, Pascal argues, they simultaneously turn away from their purpose, leading her to become desolate. Our ultimate purpose in life is happiness, which can only be found in the heart's yearning for God. Pascal goes as far as arguing, "All men are in search of happiness. There's no exception to this, whatever different methods are employed."[43] The only true process of finding happiness, Pascal argues, is to acknowledge what fails to bring true happiness and,

[42] Ibid. 89.
[43] Levering, *Proofs of God,* 108

through this revelation, turn towards what brings about this true happiness, i.e., God. In this process, the individual will find herself attempting to find happiness in finite things. To abandon faith in times of hard trials, like a pandemic, would be to abandon the pursuit of true happiness. Following this lack of faith, the individual would become fixated on filling the void of God with happiness in materials and objects, allowing herself to replace an irreplaceable love with earthbound pleasure or incomplete happiness.

I believe Pascal and I would have similar arguments concerning Montaigne, especially with regard to wavering faith. Pascal would most likely argue that a wavering faith is a sign of weakness and a natural byproduct of the human condition. To truly find happiness in God, ontotheological proofs mean little compared to what and where one's heart leads her to. The heart is what will allow us to love and find God and guides one's relationship with Him. In Montaigne's case, it sounds as if the hearts of those who lack God are deficient in the sense that they do not love God or recognize God as happiness, and therefore their faith is ready to jump ship following Luther's arguments. Our lack of necessity in the universe aids in the proof that love has its place, as does happiness. Pascal reminds us that we only find purpose in God with the heart, and through this, we can be guided through everything, including "...with the appalling necessity of being either annihilated or wretched for all eternity."[44] In short, we can choose to follow the love of God and, in doing so, find the truest form of happiness. This would demand the acceptance of God and would call upon the individual to pursue God in order to reach the highest happiness. On the other hand, the individual could fail to recognize God and be guided by a less-than-perfect happiness.

Aquinas

Aquinas asserts that one recognizes their inherent desire for God as their final end through intimate and personal knowledge of God.[45] As Pascal reasons that finding the highest happiness is analogous to finding God, Aquinas recognizes because God is the source of all things good and all knowledge, God himself is what orients the individual towards her ultimate end. Thus, for Aquinas, the pursuit of the good only requires

---

[44] Levering, *Proofs of God,* 109
[45] Levering, *Proofs of God,* 61.

"finite likenesses of God's goodness,"[46] in addition to the natural desire for God. Relating again to Pascal, the heart embraces God's goodness and love, enabling this pursuit of the good.

In his earlier writings, Aquinas argues that the nature of a being cannot be its own cause since an object's nature is distinct from its existence, since "every essence or quiddity can be understood without knowing anything about its being (*esse,* act of being). I can know, for instance, what a man or a phoenix is and still be ignorant of whether it actually exists."[47] Only by establishing the actuality of a given thing by observing its own act of existence, received externally from another source, which must have existed before it, can one determine whether something exists. Because one cannot cause one's own existence, one can always assume that if something exists, there must be some external, or separate, cause of its existence. The argument here is that whatever gives existence to something else, in turn, received its existence from something that existed prior to it.[48]

Aquinas argues, however, that there must be a singularity of existence because the transmission of

---

[46] Ibid.
[47] Levering, *Proofs of God*, 58.
[48] Argument from motion

existence from one caused being to another cannot go infinitely, as this would entail the same logical problem Damascene identifies. An infinite regression cannot account for what brings about this chain of existential causation, leading Aquinas to conclude the very nature of existential causation entails the existence of an uncaused upon a reality "whose nature is its act of being"[49] and that there can only be one such reality.[50]

Aquinas then posits that objects come into and out of existence, which can exist or not at any given time, yet there cannot be a spontaneous creation from nothing. This is indicative that something must have existed, which for Aquinas, is God.[51] Aquinas then argues that a hierarchy of goodness in things increases in complexity as the hierarchy advances. For instance, inorganic matter has a certain goodness to it, but above this are basic biological organisms, humans, etc.[52] Finally, Aquinas argues that there is an intricate structure and order to the universe, and by following the logic of the previously mentioned arguments, the entity responsible for being must be divinely intelligent.[53]

---

[49] Ibid. 59.
[50] Argument from efficient cause
[51] Argument from necessary being
[52] Argument from gradation
[53] Argument from design

Aquinas refers to these five arguments as the five proofs that logically demonstrate God's existence.

The fundamental arguments presented here regarding the nature of God serve as the foundation of what infused courage may build upon, as well as how theistic belief may better aid the courageous agent during the COVID-19 pandemic. Overall, the existence of God is entailed by the objectivity of the good, yet human reason lacks the ability to comprehend God's nature since He rests above experience. The arguments of Pascal presented in this section will be further addressed in regard to how one may overcome this inability of human reason to acknowledge God and why the practical entailments of Pascal's argument serve the individual best in terms of loving others. The following section will discuss reason, the flaws of reason, and how reason cannot grasp God in His entirety.

CHAPTER THREE

Reason and the Call to God

The divine revelation of the Gospels and Old Testament conforms to human capability to reason, yet what makes revelation unique to the human condition is its inaccessibility, which drives the endeavor to aim towards the good. However, the essential nature of God is not comprehensible to human reason. Any attempt to reduce God to a manifestation subject to one's rational comprehension is idolatrous since this erroneous perception of God is grounded in limited knowledge and experience, whereas God is an all-encompassing being, and thus His nature is inaccessible to human reason. This perplexes many Catholics since it is only reasonable that one comes to know who is on the other side of their fears, hopes, and love. Yet, this definition of God as an all-encompassing being is not conducive to understanding His nature via reason, which is why Pascal affirms that the heart finds and loves God, not reason, as discussed in the previous discussion. Pascal then suggests that loving God should be the foundation of our worship of Him rather than an all-encompassing study of His divine nature.

Pascal's justification that the heart is what influences one to follow God is further reinforced by a philosophical account of human reasons' inability to comprehend God, who is beyond our human experience. The difficulty with human reason, Kant argues, is that God is above, or outside, of our experience, as mentioned above, and so we can neither prove nor disprove God's existence through theoretical reasoning. This point supports Pascal's argument that it must not be the mind and reason but the heart that feels and experiences God fully.[54] The greater intention of this characterization is to facilitate the pursuit of the good, allowing for a greater relationship with God since His nature is love, and so He loves above all else.

---

[54] Numerous discussions with Dr. Christopher Fremaux afforded me much of the information regarding Kant and his ideas of reason.

The essential discussion then centers on how one may come to know God. Yet if God is not comprehensible via human reason or subject to human experience, how can one come to know anything about God? For Christians, Christ represents the best answer to this question, allowing for a practical approach to care for others, of repentance, and of peace. The depiction of Christ in the gospels illustrates how the knowledge of God becomes humanly accessible through Christ, in which His example is relatable to both the human condition and its faults, but it also demonstrates how one may come to know God through Christ's love. Christ's love was demonstrated by His suffering on the cross, characterized by pain and agony, but in addition to physical pain, Christ cried out, "My God, my God, why have you forsaken me?"[55] This cry out is indicative of emotional distress, which only humans are subject to, furthering Christ's depiction of the love of God and how one may come to follow in Christ's example. In short, the larger purpose of Christ's life was to establish how we may find God, the ultimate good; by humbling Himself, preaching and loving, and ultimately suffering

[55] Matthew 27:46

death for the sake of humanity, Christ sets an example of courage and love, which we are meant to follow.

Knowing God

Augustine[56] suggests God created humans for Himself so that we may seek to love Him.[57] As discussed above, one develops faith and trust in God by following Christ's example of loving others. By looking at the order of the universe, seeking the good of others, and witnessing Christ's love for us, one begins to understand God as an all-loving being. Christ did not preach for the righteous, but for sinners who acknowledge their humanity, that they have done wrong and have failed to love as God does. Loving others as God does allows for an intimate relationship with Him and further guides one to the good. Because human reason is unable to grasp God His entirety by definition, when one attempts to use theoretical reasoning to fathom God, she will end up (1) condensing the nature of God into her limited perception and understanding, (2) establishing an improper, incomplete, and idolatrous image of God, and therefore (3) she will lack a proper

---

[56] 354-430
[57] Levering, *Proofs of God*, 40.

understanding of the objective good and truth to be found in God. This can then confirm Pascal's argument, as mentioned above, yet the relationship between God and love must be discussed in order to lay the foundational principles of how one may come to be in a relationship with God. Augustine's argument then demonstrates that God is all-loving, noting human dependency upon God and that all truth comes from God. However, if God is an all-loving being, then there should be no pain and suffering, yet it still exists; so how can God be all-loving yet allow us to suffer?

Suffering and Love

On a fundamental level, just as the universe and the earth break down over time, humans must as well, since everything bound in time is subject to its effects, including decay.[58] In addition, the price of human awareness, of love and reason, is to feel pain when one becomes distressed.[59] From a biological perspective, pain calls for recognizing potential dangers and recognizing how or where these dangers may present

---

[58] Cottingham, *Why Believe?*, 147.
[59] Ibid.

again in the future. Pain then enables one to survive because it allows us to avoid dangers that may compromise survival chances. By using these biological instincts, humans (and animals) become adept in nature in order to survive, yet this account does not recognize pain inflicted by others, which demands attention.

Because love does not directly tackle all evil, a moral dilemma arises: the persistent presence of evil, even in the face of love, can discourage one from confidence in God. Where evil is caused by man, it appears that sin stains the world with evil; yet when suffering is naturally caused, what, or who, is to blame? If pain or evil originates outside human control, if its causes are natural, then it has no *moral* cause. The moral case presented in the book of Job illustrates the point that suffering may lack meaning since there is no direct answer from God to Job as to why his suffering was just. This lack of a response or justification from God leaves the question unanswered, and therefore, it takes faith to conclude that sometimes suffering has no cause. Hence, the problem of suffering reinforces the fact that reason is unable to provide a complete account of God and our relationship with Him. If pain is inflicted by another person, this has a definitive moral cause. In this case, given the circumstances of free will, we are subject to the brokenness of the human condition, the broken creation. It was never intended to include pain or death prior to the original justice in Eden, yet free will condemns man to his own will. If one is guided by God and the good, their free will becomes aligned with that of God's intended purpose for us, to love Him and others. On the other hand, ignorance of the good demonstrates the brokenness of the human condition, as mentioned above, which specifically refers to the will aimed at things other than the goodness and love of God.

Love during the pandemic may be exemplified in numerous ways that encompass the points addressed here. Exemplification of love will be addressed further, characterizing how this exemplification betters the individual and the communal response to the pandemic, which aims to shed light on a world saturated with darkness and despair. Many may argue that if such a God exists, surely, He could not allow for the suffering of so many people. To reiterate here, everyone must die, and this is inevitable, and the course of an illness is purely natural; while war calls for the execution of opposing forces, a virus has no conscious ability to choose the good—it just *is*. Because the COVID-19 virus is a natural object without the ability to pursue the good, it therefore has a natural cause. Despite this, people still suffer, and many may demand that despite this natural cause of evil, God should not allow people to suffer. The nature of suffering is far too extensive to encompass in this discussion, but the principal argument to be made here in regard to the nature of suffering rests upon one's ability to look to the good despite an evil presence; when one maintains one's sights on the good, it eventually comes to fruition, in this life or the next. In short, the virus has no morality and therefore has no moral cause, making it a natural pain outside of human control. The way in which one responds to this hinges upon her ability to recognize and act upon the good by recognizing humans as the broken creation and choosing to act in accordance with the good.

CHAPTER FOUR

The Structure of Virtue

So far, the nature of God has been discussed, and from this, the nature of God and the good are demonstrated here as pertaining fundamentally to the virtues. The virtues, by definition, are achieved through the mediation of repeated behavior with the individual's aim ordered towards the good.[60] To begin, the underpinnings of virtue will be discussed, followed by a consideration of the cardinal virtues, as understood by Aristotle and Aquinas. Since there are numerous interpretations and characterizations of virtue, it is first appropriate to survey the progression and patterns of thought concerning virtue, specifically its roots in

---

[60] Aristotle, Martin Otswald, *Nicomachean Ethics*, Book 2, §6.

philosophical thought. This will serve as the underpinnings of the subsequent discussion on more specific accounts of virtue, namely the cardinal virtues and the virtue of courage.

In his essay "The nature of the virtues," Alasdair MacIntyre raises the question of what underlies the different philosophical accounts of virtues across history. The fundamental question proposed by MacIntyre explores the problem of different characterizations of virtue, specifically the possibility that these differences could oppose one another or have different generalizations, such that the core concept of virtue becomes obscured. By comparing many of the most widely accepted perspectives, MacIntyre first illustrates that while varied conceptions of virtue prevent any common universal characterization, they nevertheless emphasize that principal features of different accounts of virtue seem to underlie all accounts, features such as their relationship to practices, habituation, and societal norms[61]. While MacIntyre goes into far more detail in his discussion, this section will emphasize similarities and differences between Aristotelean and Thomistic virtue, namely, to emphasize the evolution of Aristotelean thought into the

---

[61] Ibid. 29.

foundations of Catholicism, as well as highlight the mechanisms of virtue in both accounts and how these come into practice in the virtuous agent.

Aristotelean Virtue

The Aristotelean framework locates virtues between two extremes, namely excess and deficiency. In the case of courage, the deficiency is cowardice, and the excess is recklessness. But to practice proper virtue in accordance with reason, one must find the mean between excess and deficiency, in this case cowardice and recklessness. The ability to discern between these ends is formed through a habituation of feeling pleasure and pain at the correct things at the right time.[62] When one is able to properly feel pain and pleasure in the right manner, towards the right things, and with proper reason, then this is the mark of the mean and therefore the mark of virtuous behavior.[63]

The principal idea of virtue enables one to pursue the good, and Aristotle notes the highest good must be perfect and final, denoting that the aim of our

---

[62] Aristotle, Otswald, *Nicomachean Ethics*, Book 2, §3.
[63] Ibid. Book 2, §6.

existence is reflected in the pursuit of this highest good.[64] This highest good must be the act of happiness since, when reason is practiced in accord with virtue, the aim will always be happiness. All actions in accord with reason and virtue reflect the act of happiness since one chooses to perform actions that lead to happiness, and she doesn't choose to be happy by doing things.[65] In other words, an agent performs actions conducive to happiness, which is the final end or *telos* of human life. The *telos*, according to Aristotle, is "an activity of the soul in conformity with a rational principle..."[66] The ultimate good that one pursues must therefore be happiness in accord with reason.

Aristotelean virtue requires habituation over time for behavior to be considered virtuous, as mentioned earlier in this discussion. Such habituations train one to act promptly, consistently, and easily in a way that leads one to the ultimate good. In this way, virtues enable one to act well "by second nature." Typically, this is regarding some good internal to a communal practice, and as MacIntyre argues, such goods are the end goal of virtue rather than external goods such as money, power, or glory.[67] Learning to

---

[64] Ibid. Book 1, §7.
[65] Ibid.
[66] Ibid.

play the piano for the enjoyment that comes from it is far greater than learning to play the piano for an external motivator, like fame or wealth. MacIntyre notes that both external and internal goods involve elements of competition to excel, but internal goods are motivated by bettering the communal good of those who take part in the practice requiring a given virtue.[68] The larger point to be made is that no matter the light in which virtue is examined, certain defining characteristics discern it from other conceptions of "right action."

The foundations of virtue are built upon mediation between extremes for the sake of attaining the highest good through the gradual habituation of the soul by means of repeated actions. As MacIntyre argues, there are numerous accounts and definitions of virtue; however, the Aristotelean framework sets the foundations for Thomas Aquinas's approach, which will now be discussed.

---

[67] MacIntyre, "The Nature of the Virtues," 30.
[68] Ibid. 32.

Thomistic Virtue

Thomas Aquinas[69] builds upon Aristotle's account of four foundational virtues, which he calls "the cardinal virtues" (from the Latin *cardo,* meaning "hinge"). These virtues are prudence, justice, courage, and temperance, and they are considered "cardinal" because every virtue in some way "hinges" upon them. Indeed, every virtuous act typically requires the presence of each of these dispositions insofar as every act of virtue reflects a right order of (1) reason, (2) social relationships, (3) dangers or difficulties, and (4) natural appetites. This discussion pertaining to Thomistic virtue begins with the structure of prudence, which enables the individual to perceive the world through a vision focused on truth, structurally fostering rectitude of the will and allowing one to take the correct action and make an unerring judgment.[70] In his writings, Aquinas employs the metaphor of vision is employed frequently, namely with respect to prudence, contending that virtue is only proper when the purity of the eye successfully removes obstacles that impede its ability to focus on the good.[71]

---

[69] 1225-1274
[70] McKay, *The Infused and Acquired Virtues in Aquinas' Moral Philosophy,* 89.
[71] Ibid.

Prudence for Aquinas then closely empowers the virtuous agent in her pursuit by removing obstacles or obstructions of the good, enabling her to act upon right judgments properly informed by the will.[72]

Aquinas views the highest end of the moral life as the perfection of the self-made possible through the indwelling of the Holy Spirit, facilitated by the infused moral and theological virtues, which directs the agent towards God. The infused moral virtues are gifted to the agent from the Holy Spirit alongside the theological virtues.[73] They represent grace's transformation of the cardinal virtues so that they may now be directed not only toward natural happiness but to supernatural beatitude. In short, infused virtues involve the unique influence of the Holy Spirit, and when one receives infused virtue, God then works through the agent through the light of His grace. The three theological virtues—faith, hope, and charity—inform the agent's pursuit of the four cardinal virtues—prudence, justice, courage, and temperance—so as to direct them toward God Himself. On the other hand, the theological virtues also aid the agent in pursuing the natural goods that the cardinal virtues typically aim for. Functionally, the

[72] Ibid. 90.
[73] Ibid. 2-3.

cardinal virtues allow her to pursue the goods of human life, whereas the theological virtues orient this pursuit to an even higher good, namely eternal happiness with God.

As this discussion is centered around infused virtue, attention to the theological virtues will be limited by focusing namely on charity, as it represents the highest virtue for Aquinas since it encompasses all the moral virtues, allowing the agent to be closer in friendship with God. Most fundamentally, charity enables the agent to form a friendship with God. Further, charity, as the principal theological virtue, guides the agent to perfect the expression of the cardinal virtues.[74] Therefore, when charity is expressed as a robust and genuine virtue, it allows the agent to be directed toward the good of happiness in God, not a human good that would be imperfect.[75] Aquinas notes that this foretaste of perfect happiness is still far from its final perfect state, which we may only obtain after this life. Since charity is a theological virtue given by the Holy Spirit, Aquinas concludes that the cardinal virtues provide a preliminary frame of the final end of every act, and in this way, charity perfects our every act by

---

[74] Konyndyk De Young. "Power made Perfect in Weakness," 151.
[75] Lu Qiaoying. "Aquinas's Transformation of the Virtue of Courage," *Frontiers of Philosophy in China* 8, no.3 (2013): 482.

defining the ultimate end toward which they are directed.[76]

The natural virtues grant man to act in accord with what is naturally good, whereas the infused virtues call for habituation towards the enjoyment of the supernatural good. The virtuous agent allows her passions to become guided by reason to actively pursue the perfecting components of nature.[77] Infused virtues are not formed through moral education in a manner like the acquired virtues, yet despite this, the reception of grace enables one to strengthen infused virtue through practice and habituation with divine assistance.[78] Aquinas will argue that the acquired and infused virtues seek a different means of attaining virtue, and so the balance of excess and deficiency in each case may differ.[79] This makes sense, as the acquired virtues are formed through habituation that perfects natural goods, where the infused virtues are bestowed upon the agent directly from God, and the grace of God will continue as long as the agent has not committed a mortal sin. Specifically,

---

[76] Konyndyk De Young. "Power made Perfect in Weakness," 151.
[77] Patrick Clark."Is Martyrdom Virtuous? An Occasion for Rethinking the Relation of Christ and Virtue in Aquinas," *Journal of the Society of Christian Ethics* 30, no.1 (2010): 142.
[78] Konyndyk De Young. "Power made Perfect in Weakness," 175.
[79] McKay, *The Infused and Acquired Virtues in Aquinas' Moral Philosophy*, 64.

the infused virtues being granted to the agent is dependent on God, who is their ultimate source and can readily withdraw them from the agent.[80] Most fundamentally, however, is the difference between the perfection of natural human powers through the acquired virtues, and the power of the agent bestowed with the divine gifts. The infused virtues give the agent strength to struggle and to surrender the will completely to God, which enables the agent to resist the temptations of sin and disposes herself purely to the good. Christ again represents the clearest example of the virtuous agent, who frees mankind from sin and shines the light upon the dark, along with Mary, who differs from Christ insofar as she is not divine and requires grace for her acts of infused virtue, and Mary in this state of requiring grace unlike Christ since He is source then allows for two examples of virtuous agents, Christ not requiring divine grace and Mary who does.[81]

Aquinas argues that pleasure is essential to both infused and acquired virtue, except in the case of courage, which typically does not elicit pleasure. However, the infused virtues exist with a stronger intensity by consuming the entire agent, allowing her to

---

[80] Ibid. 66.
[81] Ibid. 71.

radiate the good through her virtuous behaviors with greater power than the agent without divine intervention.[82] Often the agent chooses to remain steadfast in her difficulty, which is not conducive to pleasure in itself, and often, this pursuit is directly contradictory to pleasure.[83] The true brilliance of the infused virtues allows for the agent to be repulsed by sin since the infused virtues tear down the pleasure found in sin.[84]

The Virtuous Agent and COVID

The exhibition of virtue during the COVID-19 pandemic will be further explored; however, attention will be briefly paid to the fundamental point of how virtue enables the agent to flourish and act in accordance with reason to best aid in her pursuit of the good. Lockdown measures certainly have the tendency to cause depression or other mental health distresses, likely due to isolation amidst a global health crisis.[85] In

---

[82] Ibid. 85.

[83] Ibid. 73.

[84] McKay, *The Infused and Acquired Virtues in Aquinas' Moral Philosophy*, 74.

[85] Jagdish Khubchandani et. Al, "Post-lockdown depression and anxiety in the USA during the COVID-19 pandemic," *Journal of Public Health* 43, no.2 (2021).

this difficult situation, the exhibition of virtue enables the individual to seek the good, where this occurs through habituation with the acquired virtues and through divine grace with the infused virtues.

Acquired virtue will enable the agent to pursue the good through the habituation of virtuous behaviors, which begins prior to the pandemic and should continue through its duration. While this exhibition may not involve martyrdom, the same principals apply. In terms of infused virtue, prayer serves as a conversation between the individual and God, and when accompanied by acquired virtues, it induces her to do great work during the pandemic. In both forms of virtue, helping others is a clear example of virtue, yet with infused virtue, the grace of God enables her to overcome adversity in order to achieve the good, which is clearly defined through this friendship with God.

In short, virtue enables her to do good despite the obstacles she may encounter. While acquired virtue can only be effective if a pattern of habituation has already been in place, with infused virtue, the grace of God enables her to act virtuously towards the ultimate end of the good without the necessity of habituation. The equivalent of habituation in the infused virtues is clearly seen in performing virtuous actions, defined by the good, to further her love of God. COVID will be further analyzed once a clearer picture, namely with courage, has been established.

CHAPTER FIVE

Courage

This section serves to offer a contrast between the Thomistic approach to the classical Aristotelean perspective. A contrast between these accounts highlights the implications of courage, namely the theistic approach, which will better serve the agent during COVID-19. Fundamentally, the comparisons drawn demonstrate the similarity and evolution of the Aristotelean framework to the foundations of Catholicism, specifically Aquinas's approach to virtue ethics. Subsequently, Aquinas will deem God to be a fundamental source of virtue, as mentioned above, which perfects the rational agent's aims towards the good. Aquinas and Aristotle's concept of the good will be compared, with a particular focus on Aquinas's approach to virtue ethics. Primarily, the Thomistic approach to the good and perfection of the soul will be built upon Aristotelean ideals yet maintains much clearer accuracy in its aim, as the Aristotelean perspective recognizes that actualization of happiness is the final perfect end, despite both recognizing that happiness is in accordance with the moral agent and her soul. Following this, the virtues and how they allow the agent to arrive at this ultimate stage of happiness will provide a necessary framework for the agent. Here, the key differences between natural and infused virtues and natural and cardinal virtues will be compared.

The foundations of courage are informed by prudence and justice. Specifically, the nature of courage calls for the confrontation of a difficulty that obscures the vision or attainment of the good. Aquinas discusses that an act of courage consists of two components: endurance and aggression. Further, these individual components will be analyzed and discussed, highlighting the importance of endurance in acts of courage. This discussion will entail an analysis of virtue, which lays the groundwork for discerning courage as an act of virtue. The natures of both justice and prudence will then be examined in order to discern and distinguish the foundations of courage, which allows it to be a force for the pursuit of the good. This section specifically discusses the Thomistic structure of courage. In this view, one exhibits courage if and only if one properly exhibits prudence and justice as well, since courage calls for practical wisdom and the bettering of the community, respectively. Both the Thomistic and Aristotelean accounts of courage and virtue align here. However, the key differences between the two accounts deals with (1) who can be considered courageous in the Thomistic account versus the Aristotelean and (2) the relative importance of aggression and endurance in acts of courage.

The Cardinal Virtues

Prudence is the most fundamental virtue since it informs all others by ordering the intellect towards the attainment of the good and by regulating the development and attainment of knowledge of the good, aiding in an agent's ability to flourish. More specifically, prudence orders the intellect toward attaining the good, allowing for a development of knowledge of the good, enabling her to act decisively with a purpose towards the good. The ultimate end of prudence, then, is to dispose one to employ practical reason in the pursuit of the good. Both the Aristotelean and Thomistic accounts recognize prudence as governing the ability to properly aim at the good by means of developing knowledge of the good. Similarly, both Aquinas and Aristotle contend that prudence is the highest of the natural virtues as it is acquired through habituation, which directs the intellect and the will towards the good. As prudence aligns the intellect towards the good most fundamentally, the foundations of prudence must be examined since it informs the exhibition of justice and courage. Specifically, attention will be given to the exemplification of prudence in the face of the COVID-19 pandemic and how it informs courageous action, as well as how prudence disposes the agent to act in accord with justice.

Perception and evaluation allow for prudence to govern the agent to discern what actions may be called for. In this sense, the ability of the agent to correctly perceive the situation, followed by a proper evaluation, permits the agent to first identify a context that calls for prudence and, second, guides the agent to process the correctly identified situation. Prudence will then make the agent habituated towards thinking and acting in accordance with the intellect, again to be aimed at the good. Prudence then enables the implementation of the other virtues and allows our emotions to be oriented toward the good.[86] When emotions are ordered toward the good, the individual can respond to this hypothetical scenario with appropriate virtue. However, the extent of prudence in this discussion does not permit its true virtuous capabilities since allowing the manifestation of prudence in the virtuous agent in practice trumps a mere conversation. In other words, stipulating the range of prudence in a discussion is far less accurate than placing it into practice, allowing the virtuous agent to become habituated to acting prudently.

Since prudence is manifested when the agent uses her situational awareness and facts of the situation, given by proper evaluation and perception, subsequent actions then become aimed at the good. Justice then will allow the agent to utilize the powers of the soul to preserve and cultivate the relationships necessary for flourishing. Aristotle regards justice as one of the highest exemplifications of virtue since he argues that justice encapsulates all other virtues,[87] namely by

---

[86] Darnell et. Al. "A Multifunction Approach to Assessing Aristotelian Phronesis (Practical Wisdom)." *Personality and Individual Differences* 196, (2022): 3.

respecting justice as a high form of excellence, following that those who act in accord with justice utilize their capabilities to better the good for others, yet argues that giving attention to the common good does not trump pursuing the good for the individual; rather, seeking good for oneself is *compatible* with seeking the good for the community. For instance, dying on the battlefield represents both courageous and just action. However, in this example, only justice will be considered; the just act of sacrificing oneself for the community (1) involves the agent aiming their actions to defend the community, and (2) represents the glory and great good that the agent achieves. Therefore, when the agent aims their actions at the good of the community in death in battle, the agent exemplifies justice as well as prudence.

Similar to Aristotle's account, the *Catechism of the Catholic Church* defines justice as "the moral virtue that consists in the constant and firm will to give their due to God and neighbor."[88] Here, the virtuous act is considered not solely based on whether the individual aims at bettering the community but rather on whether the individual seeks to serve God and, thereby, the community because a love in God is built upon loving

---

[87] Aristotle, Otswald, *Nicomachean Ethics*, Book 5, §1.
[88] *Catechism of the Catholic Church*, 2nd ed., 1807.

others. In both accounts presented, justice is the virtue responsible for enabling the individual to better communities, including active and purposeful participation in which the agent aims to perfect the whole because she also depends on that good, forming a unique relationship between the agent and her community. As all virtuous behavior is, justice is aimed at the good because it seeks to love God; this love of God, in turn, requires serving others and furthering their ability to flourish and pursue the good. We cannot consider justice without looking beyond human experience since nothing in our realm of being truly encapsulates justice; only when the aim is at God, above experience, is justice truly exemplified since it calls for a regard for God *and* others.

Justice is often exemplified by combating systemic injustices, and calling for rectification of unjust practices increases equity for all. For instance, issues of color or race are seen as hallmarks of injustice, where the solution calls for equity for all races. During COVID-19, proper justice could be exemplified by avoiding excess in the supermarkets or other supplies and focusing on helping others in some way. These COVID-specific challenges demonstrate justice since the tendency to protect and provide for family or friends so that others may get a fair share of masks, sanitizers, toilet paper, etc., must be governed, in a sense counterintuitive to what may be typically deemed prudent.[89] Rules and laws can only be so effective in COVID. For example, to prevent uneven distributions of supplies, rather those upholding the virtue of justice are far more vital in promoting the flourishing of a community than being ruled or instructed by law; when justice is chosen out of free will, compared to legislation or some other ruling, flourishing is far more commonplace because *hearts* collectively aim at the pursuit of the good. Justice aims at more than just obeying the law since it may be deemed to fight what is common practice or lawful if it is not aimed at the good.

The exhibition of courage follows the proper embodying of justice and prudence, as these virtues align the will in a way that follows the good in accordance with reason of the will. Thus, the full possession of courage depends upon the full development of prudence and justice. In other words, prudence and justice give rise to any true form of courage.[90] However, it should be noted that justice

---

[89] Fowers, Novak, Calder, & Sommer. "Courage, Justice, and Practical Wisdom as Key Virtues in the Era of COVID-19," *Frontiers in Psychology* 12, (2021): 3.

[90] Josef Pieper, *The Four Cardinal Virtues: Prudence, Justice, Fortitude,*

differs significantly from courage; whereas justice *typically* follows norms and laws, courage goes beyond this. The courageous agent has no difficulty responding to calls for justice, even if it breaks norms or law. Following that, prudence informs courage by mediating recklessness and cowardice; the act of virtue eliminates and enables proper reactions to present challenges. This regulation of cowardice and recklessness orients the agent toward virtue in accord with reason, and when this behavior is deemed to be neither reckless nor cowardly, as informed by the will and reason, only then can this behavior be deemed prudent. Following prudence, justice enables for the good for others, which thereby facilitates courage to benefit others, as well as the individual agent; however, the definition of courage calls upon the virtuous agent attempting courageous behavior to sacrifice for the greater good in some capacity, while evaluating and giving proper acknowledgment to the present evil or challenge. In short, prudence orients the agent towards the mean between recklessness and cowardice, and justice orients the agent to the good of the community as well as the good for themselves. By this, the virtuous agent

Temperance. Twentieth Century Religious Thought (University of Notre Dame Press, 2010), 123.

58

flourishes by doing good for others by following the dispositions of the will towards the good.

Exemplification of Courage

Following the discussion above, exemplification of courage occurs in a scenario in which one must discern how much risk is appropriate and how to best respond to this appropriate amount of risk, enabling and calling for endurance in the face of evil.[91] A proper exemplification of courage maintains, by means of virtue, a mean between cowardice and recklessness in a given situation. With courage as an act of virtue, there must be a mediation between two opposing calls of the agent, fear, and assurance, since the definition of virtue calls for mediation most fundamentally. Notably, fear does not rule out the possibility of courage, as fear must exist for a given behavior to be considered courageous. Further, fear *and* recklessness in the agent must be present because the principal act of virtue is the means of mediation by the will in order for the agent's actions to be aimed at the good. This intricate balance can only be deemed courageous when the desired outcome is

---

[91] Peter Greach, *The Virtues* (Cambridge University Press, 1977), 150.

aimed at the good and when fear is present in some capacity, yet the individual acts despite their fear so as to pursue the good.[92] The amount of fear and assurance to be exercised is determined by the agent evaluating the given situation, and this process is driven by the agent's desire for the good, allowing them to act in accordance with reason.

To reiterate, the purpose of regulating fear or recklessness is to pursue the good. Moderating two extremes for the sake of the good, as in the case of courage, allows us to consider the action virtuous. In the specific instance of courage, two conditions must be met, the first being that fear and assurance are regulated by reason and the second being that for an act to be courageous, it must be aimed at pursuing the good.

Aquinas discerns different degrees of courage, beginning at a fundamental and more ordinary level and leading up to its highest form in martyrdom.[93] The primary degree of courage is routinely exemplified in daily life and enables one to pursue a higher degree, which Aquinas refers to as infused courage, enabling the Christian to listen to God and to hand over control completely to Him.[94] This change takes a considerable

---

[92] Aristotle, Otswald, *Nicomachean Ethics*, Book 3, §7.
[93] Pieper, *The Four Cardinal Virtue*, 136.
[94] Ibid. 138.

amount of courage since there can be a great amount of fear present, but once attained, we can better love God and pursue the good. Again, what makes this surrender to God challenging is that one must relinquish control, and in this moment, trust that God may grab hold of one's hand. Surrendering fears and anxieties to God better enables the individual to pursue the good and love others. The highest degree of courage for Aquinas is martyrdom, when one relinquishes not only their soul and heart but their very existence to God for the sake of the highest good. However, the fundamental difference between the Thomistic and Aristotelean accounts of virtue lies in Aquinas defining the perfection of the human agent to be reliant upon the grace of God driving charity. This overview of the Thomistic approach to virtue will be further discussed in greater detail.

Significance and Implications of Courage

With the foundations of courage presented, we can therefore derive its meaning and significance. Courage is ultimately concerned with death, and the utmost exemplification of courage is a self-sacrifice, in which one willingly accepts death in order to serve his or her community in some capacity, and according to Aristotle, all courage is driven by the fear of death.[95] The nature of death consists namely of the loss of what is good in the face of what is unknown since when one is courageous, one must love life to risk it for the good. Because for Aristotle, there can be no lasting good or evil for the dead, and beyond death, nothing can be certain. Risking death for the sake of the good represents the highest form of courage, similar to Aquinas's arguments pertaining to martyrdom.[96] Specifically, the highest exemplification of courage for Aristotle is during war or when one dies for a noble cause since it is in such circumstances that one's excellence is most clearly exemplified.[97]

In short, courage enables us to realize the rational good by enabling us to pursue it despite the fears that might divert or discourage us from seeking it.[98] The highest exemplification of courage is seen in the martyr, characterized by their willingness to die for the sake of the good and so overcome the most fundamental aversion we have, namely our aversion to

---

[95] Aristotle, Otswald, *Nicomachean Ethics*, Book 3, §6.
[96] Clark, "Is Martyrdom Virtuous?," 143.
[97] Ibid.
[98] Konyndyk De Young, "Power made Perfect in Weakness," 157.

death.[99] Martyrs best exemplify courage because they confront their challenge despite the fear they feel in the presence of the most fatal of all harms so as to maintain their pursuit of the good. On a more fundamental level, prudence and justice allow the courageous individual to mediate fear and confidence rationally to better pursue the common good of the community. The larger idea at hand is that the exhibition of courage aids in the confrontation and endurance of what is most fearful, including a global pandemic.

---

[99] Clark, "Is Martyrdom Virtuous?," 148.

CHAPTER SIX

Infused Courage

The specific role of courage is to preserve the good by removing obstacles that inhibit the agent's ability to reason properly. Courage can then be viewed as the ability of the soul to endure difficulty, most fundamentally death.[100] In this way, courage enables the individual to be sustained against fear when pursuing the good, which calls for her to live in accord with the Truth, specifically exemplified through Christ's self-sacrifice.[101] The challenge then becomes how to determine whether an act is truly courageous. Aristotle proposes that only if the danger presents the possibility of a noble death can an act be considered courageous, and for this reason, Aristotle notes that the soldier's

---

[100] Konyndyk De Young, "Power made Perfect in Weakness," 152
[101] Ibid. 157.

death on the battlefield represents the highest form of courage.[102] Following Aquinas's discussion of the threat of death, Aquinas deems the primary act of courage to consist in enduring a threat despite its potential capacity to obscure reason, at least temporarily.[103] Up to this point, Aristotle and Aquinas agree that the chief object of courage revolves around death. In the case of martyrdom, we are presented with two possibilities regarding the integrity of the virtuous agent, the first being that the agent is only virtuous if and only if her fears don't obscure her sight of the good or her perseverance in holding fast to it. Aquinas adds a second condition, namely that the agent must receive assistance from the Holy Spirit in order to receive the strength necessary to remain steadfast in her pursuit of the good.[104]

In his exploration of courage, Aquinas differs from Aristotle and numerous other accounts of courage by suggesting that courage is a virtue that can be exhibited not only by heroic warriors but also by the disabled, by women, by the young and the old, etc. In his account of Christian courage, anyone with the

---

[102] Clark, "Is Martyrdom Virtuous?," 143.
[103] Ibid. 144.
[104] Konyndyk De Young, "Power made Perfect in Weakness," 176.

capacity and ability to love God above all else is capable of exemplary courage.[105] The overall view of courage in the Thomistic account follows that the agent aligns her fears with the good, reinforcing her ability to stand strong in the face of challenges. Courage namely protects the agent where she is most intimate and vulnerable, namely with respect to her fear of death.[106] Courage is a response to what is good in the face of what is evil, enabling the agent to continue her pursuit in spite of its difficulty. The role of prudence and justice, then, is to allow the agent to act with regard to the will's disposition towards the good and to visualize the good in its entirety.

The Final End of Courage

Since we do not know God directly, the infused virtues given by the divine grace of the Holy Spirit allow the individual to partake in the gifts of the Holy Spirit and, ultimately, in God's own life.[107] For Aquinas, the foremost end of courage aims to facilitate spiritual warfare to allow the agent to attain heavenly Beatitude.[108]

---

[105] Konyndyk De Young, "Courage as a Christian Virtue," 310.
[106] Ibid. 303.
[107] McKay, *The Infused and Acquired Virtues in Aquinas' Moral Philosophy*, 37.
[108] Ibid. 126.

The martyr is not the only one who engages in this sort of spiritual struggle, but she nevertheless represents the clearest and most paradigmatic example of it.[109] Ultimately, the agent can pursue courage with more temporal aims in mind or towards God. Christ as the teacher of the New Law, professes that the virtuous agent infused with the grace of God is to pursue the kingdom of Heaven and to aggressively resist temptations of the devil and sin.[110] In addition to this, Aquinas finds that the virtues of humility, patience, and perseverance aid the agent in the exercise of a courageous act. Humility serves the agent by allowing her to properly recognize her insignificance, to correctly evaluate herself, and hence to pursue God's greatness rather than her own. This departs from the Aristotelian account to the extent that the humble individual recognizes her weaknesses and faults and thereby correctly appraises her own worth. The Thomistic account thus goes beyond the Aristotelian account by prioritizing the agent's recognition of her insignificance and attentiveness to the glory of God's greatness.[111] Patience allows the agent to endure some present evil or

[109] Ibid. 133.
[110] McKay, *The Infused and Acquired Virtues in Aquinas' Moral Philosophy*, 135.
[111] Ibid. 166.

discomfort, enabling her to focus less on the current challenges she faces so that she may remain focused on the higher good.[112] Perseverance allows the agent to maintain her pursuit of the good over a stretch of time, namely tied to her mental state as she pursues the good. This ties in with patience to the extent that the latter enables her to first fix herself on a future good and so to avoid things that may obscure this view, while the former continually allows her to pursue the end good.[113]

Significance of Courageous Endurance and its Perfection

For Aquinas, endurance is the chief act of courage, rather than aggression, because (1) endurance implies that the agent is attacked by someone stronger or from a greater position, whereas aggression implies the agent would be stronger over their opponent; (2) endurance enables the agent to be sustained against a present threat rather than aggression which implies for an anticipated danger; and (3) endurance implies a longer duration of challenge or threat whereas aggression implies a rather quick action against a threat.[114]

---

[112] Ibid. 167.
[113] Ibid. 180.

A particular difficulty with endurance involves sorrow acting against the agent when she endures an evil; anger and courage, on the other hand, reinforce aggression. Because of this, the enduring agent must engage in an internal struggle between emotions, whereas the agent acting with aggression may make use of emotion against the aggressor.[115] This internal struggle creates much difficulty for the agent, and, in turn, this is where the courage in the deed is found, specifically in the endurance of the difficulty and her ability to remain steadfast and motivated towards the good.

The ultimate perfection of courage in the individual is most fundamentally driven by the framework of the human condition itself, in which reasoning gives rise to the philosophical life and the ability to see goods to be pursued, however distant they may be.[116] In the context of Catholicism, prayer and reflection serve as a compass for the agent to orient her towards the good. For the average individual, the good may seem more attainable on the social or political level, yet beyond this lies much more opportunity for the agent to prove her compassion and obedience for God.

---

[114] Konyndyk De Young, "Power made Perfect in Weakness," 156.
[115] Ibid. 166.
[116] Clark, *Perfection in Death*, 188.

This may not mean martyrdom per se but could include a step above practicing the faith and maintaining a relationship with God. In short, courage for Aquinas challenges the individual to love God and have their life centered around the virtues, aimed at the good. Through courage, she will be able to live the philosophical life and achieve some association with the metaphysical, allowing for an intimate reflection of the good and its pursuit in accordance with reason. Martyrdom is certainly the costliest form of courage, but numerous instances demand political forms of courage that do not lead to death. Also, if martyrdom became too common, it would call into question the very meaning of pursuing the good, thus diminishing respect for the difficulties to be endured in attaining these goods.

The implications of courage informed by God allow for "…the inner transformation of the person accomplished through grace."[117] The end goal for Aquinas then becomes for the virtues to enable the following of Christ.[118] In the next section on theistic courage, infused virtues from God will be discussed, as well as Aquinas's treatment of courage from God.

---

[117] Konyndyk De Young, "Power made Perfect in Weakness," 148.
[118] Ibid. 149.

Emphasis will be placed on how courage informed by God can better aid in courageous behavior during the COVID-19 pandemic. Accounts of courage will be examined, specifically implications of courage and how these examples bettered their communities with God providing a foundation for positive change when faith and hope run low.

The Thomistic Exemplification of Highest Courage

Aristotle's examples of courage revolve around the noble death in battle. Aquinas highlights that although martyrdom, as the highest exemplification of courage, may require physical strength, the agent still remains vulnerable, and with the aid of the Holy Spirit, the martyr's ability to maintain her sight upon the good enables the soul to remain strengthened despite the physical body's condition. Aquinas departs from the typical Aristotelian account of courage, allowing others besides the warrior on the battlefield to exemplify courage since, for Aquinas, the "...dominant model of courage is not the attacking warrior but the enduring martyr."[119] As briefly mentioned, the Thomistic approach to martyrdom does not preclude women, people with disabilities, the weak, the old, or the young, as the Aristotelean model does. Specifically, the Thomistic model portrays martyrdom in a way that allows courage to be seen far more spiritually, focusing on the relationship between the agent and God, compared to the Aristotelean model, which focuses on the warrior's courage in attack.[120]

The most direct difference between the Thomistic and Aristotelean perspectives is that Aristotle views courage chiefly as being most perfectly exemplified by noble death on the battlefield, whereas Aquinas finds that any death for the sake of the good is just as perfect and the divine grace of the Holy Spirit aids in the agent's vision remaining fixated upon the highest good.[121] Again, both agree that courage is a habit that removes the difficulties of attaining the good. Further, Aquinas and Aristotle will agree that every action, once the intellect can apprehend the good, will be motivated to achieve that good, which is driven by the sensory appetite in the soul[122].

---

[119] Clark," Is Martyrdom Virtuous?," 145.
[120] Konyndyk De Young, "Power made Perfect in Weakness," 170.
[121] Qiaoying, "Aquinas's Transformation of the Virtue of Courage," 471.
[122] Ibid. 473.

The Appetite of the Soul

The soul can find the perfection of the sensory appetites by following them in accordance with reason since reason is the determinative governing component of the soul.[123] Prudence is the virtue that will perfect the agent and her reason, just as justice will perfect her will in order to establish "the rectitude of reason."[124]

If the sensory appetite, for Aquinas, desires a good or an end not following reason, then one does not yet possess the virtue of temperance, which properly moderates the passions. The provoking of these passions, as Aquinas describes it, is the responsibility of the conducible power.[125] Courage will then be the force that enables her to act and strengthen her will, despite the fear or challenges that may be present.[126] With this being said, Aquinas and Aristotle would both agree that the ideal virtuous agent's soul takes delight in virtuous acts and that, ultimately, this delight comes from the end rather than being virtuous.[127]

---

[123] Ibid. 474.
[124] Ibid.
[125] Ibid.
[126] Ibid.
[127] Ibid. 170.

In a final comparison, natural courage calls for the agent to respond properly to a threat and remain steadfast in her pursuit of natural goods, whereas infused courage calls for this plus aiming their actions at God. Because the virtuous agent infused with the grace of God will aim her actions at God and work for the good despite the physical or mental difficulty, she will be oriented to the most perfect end. The agent, only influenced by natural virtue, lacks the ability to discern where the good emanates from, yet she is not completely lost or hopeless in terms of living the good life. If and when she aims her actions at this good, she will have the opportunity to know God during this lifetime and engage in a meaningful friendship with Him, His divine support, and infinite love.

The Necessity of Courage in God's Divine Plan

Following that theistic courage differs from the typical exhibition of courage by the grace of God guiding virtuous behavior, it is reasonable to question how this applies to following Christ.

> "I think God continually gives us clues and landmarks to help us stay on course… we may choose to ignore them, or not even notice them—all because they are not part of the plan that we've laid out for ourselves. When Jesus was born, he didn't arrive as the people expected or wanted—and so again the message or landmark was lost on many. Jesus arrived, but they missed it and walked on their way. He was just one of many births that took place that night long ago."[128]

---

[128] Fr. Richard Ricard, Christmas Homily, 2022 (St Bernard's Church, Rockville CT). I chose to use this homily since it really speaks to the path of following Christ. Following the path of God rather than one's own takes immense courage, as it requires, literally, a leap of faith to trust God.

Above is an excerpt from Fr. Richard Ricard's Christmas homily of 2022, emphasizing how Christ entered the world in such a vulnerable manner that surely, He couldn't be the redeemer of the world; Christ entered the world born amongst animals, as an infant, and poor. The manner in which Christ entered the world is opposed to how we may expect such an important person to enter the world or live. So why would the Redeemer be so vulnerable? The answer is rather simple: to be with us, the sinners, the poor, the weak, and the vulnerable. Christ practiced humility to be with us and to teach so that even the most vulnerable and poorest in society would know that God loves them and that they are not forgotten. As Fr. Rick put it, "We don't need a packed resume to get into heaven; we need to have loved, shown compassion, been faithful to God and our vocations, and been generous with our gifts."[129] The importance here is that Christ teaches that humility and love are far more important than status or prestige.

---

[129] This too comes from Fr. Richard Ricard's Christmas homily, 2022. I felt it important to include this since it ascribes the conditions in which Christ entered our world to serve the neglected of society. It took immense courage for the disciples and believers in Christ to come to this belief. Why would society, which values anything but the weak, come to worship a man who serves them and lives amongst them? Further, why would any individual believe in the Holy Divinity found in Christ when she may be comfortable already, and perhaps already aimed at the good? Fr. Rick here begins this conversation, and in my discussion on courage, serves as a brief point on courage in belief.

"Blessed are the poor in spirit," he said, "for theirs is the kingdom of heaven."[130]

One key difficulty for Christians is following the divine plan God has since it may be challenging to look for God's guidance or to follow through with this plan even if one recognizes it. The ability of infused virtue to guide the agent is granted by the Holy Spirit and enables the agent to pursue the most difficult of challenges with the added support of the Divine. Following Aquinas's definition of spiritual delight and sorrow and the function of the Holy Spirit's role in infused virtue, we can argue that the Divine aids in challenges when we are ready to give up on ourselves. When our fragile souls are struggling under pressure, God's aid enables incredible feats, whether martyrdom or following the plan given by the Father.

Infused Courage and COVID

A proper examination of theistically informed courage will allow for an examination of COVID in a light that allows for decision-making in accord with reason, informed by faith in God. One of the more

---

[130] Matthew 5:3

prominent moral dilemmas for Catholics revolves around whether COVID vaccination is moral considering that fetal cell lines were used to develop the vaccines. The cause for concern is that the vaccines were made possible by an act in which human life was disregarded. Both sides of this debate concern human life; if one should receive the vaccine, it could be argued that one's life is more valuable than that of the one who produced the fetal cell line used. We have both a moral obligation to pursue the good in accord with reason, namely, to allow for our love for others to be informed by God. Yet this logic implies both ends of the vaccine debate. We have a moral obligation to our communities and loved ones to keep them safe, as well as to respect life for what it is, a gift from God. Courage informed by faith in God is key to making this decision. With this in mind, courage informed by grace allows one to make the best decision regarding the vaccine with ease. In other words, I find both alternatives to be equally correct, and the prompting of the Holy Spirit aids the individual whenever the good at stake appears to be equally significant or equally ordered to God. Simply put, reason becomes influenced by the Holy Spirit, which enables the intellect to be ordered to the demands of the good, and how this decision regarding vaccination impacts her immediate community. This approach, informed by the Holy Spirit, allows for the individual to make a decision with the good in mind, as well as love, which therefore empowers her to make the best decision possible.

Children have been subject to higher-than-normal stress, with the shutdown of schools preventing learning, security, and interactions with other children. There is an innate responsibility of those with children to consider their best interests. Children globally have suffered in numerous ways, as schooling is essential for their development. In working to discern what is best for children, school, or COVID safety, courage can potentially pertain to both sides of the issue. Courage informed by the Holy Spirit enables a guidance towards the most moral option.

One of the more profound examples of the exhibition of theistically informed courage pertains to frontline workers, as there are numerous examples of those serving the sick who may become burned out or die from illness. This courage to serve the vulnerable is informed by the Holy Spirit, which enables those working despite the dangers of the pandemic to continue to do so. Patricia Benamon worked during the pandemic as a travel nurse and found God to be her source of comfort when she became burned out.[131] She notes that the ability to pray and find relief in God enabled her to continue her work as a nurse despite burnout.[132] In a hypothetical scenario, I would argue that an atheistic perspective of burnout would be more challenging since one would lack the rock which grounds one and the perfect source of comfort during the individual's time of need.

---

[131] Patricia Benamon. "Keeping the Faith: A Healthcare Workers Story of Burnout." (2022).
[132] Ibid.

CHAPTER SEVEN

Death and Martyrdom

The ideas and notions of death are obscure by the faults of the human condition, yet light can be shed upon death and its meaning through Christ. Death is certain, and one must die, yet the question remains: why? This discussion begins with the original notions of death in the Garden of Eden, followed by postmodern thought surrounding death. Martyrdom, in its most pure form, is the agent who gives her life for the greater good, God, by resembling in her sacrifice Christ and by the gift of infused courage is enabled to maintain her sight upon this good in her final hour. In short, death was never meant to be. Rather, it signifies the distance between creator and creation and demonstrates the reality of the gift of free will, which enables the agent to choose good. By death, we are given the opportunity to be united with Christ, or lack thereof, determined by the agent's ability to discern her gift of free will for the greater good. Following this, I begin this discussion by labeling death an opportunity since death is the great equalizer that equates one's ability to do good and to love with Christ. In the context of COVID, the agent must consistently aim her intentions and actions at the good and overcomes any barriers with the gift of infused virtue.

The Human Condition and Death: An Opportunity

The conceptualization of death represents the epitome of fear, the ultimate constraint on the human condition, and the reference point for life, recognized most evidently when living the philosophical life. The origins of death and death's implications elude our ability to reason since death resides outside of experience. The connection between death and God deserves the utmost attention, considering that from a biblical perspective, death itself is a punishment, representing the split and isolation of man from God in Eden.[133] The original conditions of justice in Eden never included death as an integral component of the human condition. This appears true since the nature of death paralyzes thought and evokes fear, which conflicts with the teachings of the Father by Christ. Rather, the threat of death must be dangerous since God never intended for death to be. The quote from the Book of Wisdom above most clearly demonstrates that God hasn't made death an integral part of His creation and does not take any pleasure in the death of any of His creatures. Death then demonstrates our severed relationship with God, namely that death serves as a barrier between the soul of the individual and immortality with the Father. Christ serves as an example of how death was not meant to be. Christ *endures* death and so holds out the opportunity for the dying to follow His example. When we suffer and die, and when we transform and resurrect, we are dying and resurrecting with Christ. Here, Christ is both the model for us to follow as well as our source of grace for transformation.[134]

What becomes difficult regarding the nature of death follows that fear is largely biological in nature, yet

[133] Clark, *Perfection in Death*, 145.
[134] Clark, "Is Martyrdom Virtuous?," 153.

the rational animal is disposed to the ultimate end, beyond which there is no foreseeable good, yet retains a far greater understanding of this inevitability than the nonrational animal. It follows that only when living are the goods known to the agent and are able to be understood as such; death, as the lack of life, entirely depletes the agent of all possible goods. Aquinas's unique position regarding death conceives of death as a "proving ground" for one's relationship with God.[135]

One such way to contemplate Christian courage is the *memento mori* process defined by Aquinas, which calls for reflection on our life in the context of our death. Here, the individual may ask questions that involve an ability to love, perseverance in faith, daily acts for others, and leaving behind a lasting impact of love.[136] Death and making meaningful attempts at embracing death thus allow one to use death as a point of reference for the good that the virtues make possible. One can view death as the ultimate horizon that puts all other acts and desires into perspective. In other words, accepting death requires an all-encompassing view of eudaimonia since death is the ultimate philosophical question begging for reflection, involving a

---

[135] Lee Yearley. "The Nature-Grace Question in the Context of Fortitude." (Thomist, 1971), 571.
[136] Konyndyk De Young, "Courage as a Christian Virtue, " 310.

methodological and teleological evaluation of one's life as a whole.[137] Besides *memento mori,* prayer draws the agent closer to God, enabling her to rely on His strength above her own to pursue the final good.[138]

An interesting approach to the death question is evaluated by Heidegger,[139] who first emphasizes that we are beings concerned with meaning and freedom, ultimately driven by death.[140] Society and culture become problematic since the call of the masses aims to disburden the individual by electing meaning for them. For Heidegger, the pressures and angst of existence drive an existential anxiety in the search for meaning, and this uncertainty of the individual allows for society to elect this meaning. The individual must then separate from the herd and look at her own mortality as an individual. This comes when death is contemplated, and during this contemplation, the individual will find herself that death ultimately individuates us, and to fully be individuated in death separate from the masses, she must summon the courage to die her own death, where you must evaluate meaning for yourself rather than obey

---

[137] Clark, *Perfection in Death*, 112.
[138] Konyndyk De Young. "Courage as a Christian Virtue," 312.
[139] 1889-1976
[140] The points presented above on Heidegger come from discussion with Dr. Duane Armitage.

societal and social pressures of meaning. Death is also certain since one must die, yet it is outstripped, meaning it is the essence of existence and most important for Heidegger. Finally, death is indefinite in its nature, as it induces existential anxiety for numerous reasons, primarily since one will not know when they will die. Heidegger's account of post-modern death is somewhat similar to Aquinas's calling for *memento mori,* namely that a careful reflection on death guides the pursuit of meaning, allowing for reflection and meditation on God and the Truth we follow in Him.

Heidegger's arguments against onto-theological metaphysics are on solid grounds for discussion. His first observation is that, as rational beings, we naturally have a desire for knowledge and to understand. His caveat to this, however, is that this pursuit of knowledge overwhelms the very act of being. This argument is sound, as he points out that wanting more or pursuing beyond our natural abilities is a flawed way to be or to live. He also points out that Christian theology aims to push aside the act of being in order to find more and attempt to get a far better understanding of the universe to the point where being itself becomes flawed and deadly. However, he does argue that the best way to understand our own being is through contemplation but concludes from this that "being is always the being of a being."[141] From this, Heidegger's key argument is that we must live on our own accord. I would argue here that this would prove that we are dependent on God because, without rationality and reason, being has no meaning. In order to be, we are dependent on a being far greater than us for universal and objective truth, God.

The key problem of this onto-theology, which calls Heidegger to conclude its innate deadliness, stems from his observation that we seek to undermine and reevaluate both meaning and being by seeking "a more original interpretation of human beings' being toward God, prescribed by the meaning of faith itself and remaining within it."[142] The basis of this argument falls on Heidegger's idea of beings' self-interest in the act of being. Because he argues that we can only understand being by being, driven by the self-interest of our own being, seeking the meaning of being in God as a faulty mechanism for self-actualization. He also argues that because being, not thinking, is the "ground that grounds[143]" the act of thinking or exploring metaphysics, including

---

[141] Levering, *Proofs of God,* 183.
[142] Ibid. 184.
[143] Ibid. 188.

onto-theology because of it being external from the self, is what makes thinking so deadly. When we replace being for the sake of being, explore its meaning internally, and seek from "external" sources, we artificially replace the primacy of being.

Because Heidegger defines the conscious as "the call of care from the uncanniness of being-in-the-world that summons Daesin [the human being] to its own most potentiality-for-being-guilty"[144] this must mean that it is the conscious that is the driving force of the being, which is also the center in which our rationality coagulates into making judgments and driving one to pursue good and truth. Specifically, with this, I see a major flaw in his line of logic; if we have a conscious according to Heidegger's definition, then we must need a reference point for deriving meaning. We cannot, without rationality and God as the objective source of truth, actively use our conscious to pursue being. It is necessary that God must be so that we can learn to derive meaning and what orients us towards morality.

I see the logic of this argument as clear. However, I believe Heidegger is missing critical information behind each of the "steps" he took to arrive

---

[144] Ibid. 185.

at this conclusion. Again, without our God-given rationality, we have no conscious to speak of, let alone the lack of free will. We cannot think rationally, as we are so designed to do, without the consciousness. In Heidegger's case, this would make the act of pursuing any good ultimately futile because there is no mechanism to derive meaning from anything. The faults of our being remain of the highest importance. When one recognizes the objective good and truth, this drives her towards God so that she may find meaning as a being with a purpose. Understanding being by being is sound; however, to be a being driven by the highest good (i.e., live with the purpose of pursuing truth and goodness) requires the ability to locate the source of these truths and look to this source for how to obtain them or how to pursue these truths. The most original interpretation of human beings can only come from God, as He is the source of all being, including consciousness and the ability to reason. If we were to exclusively look internally for the meaning of being, we would find a dead end readily, and once one reaches this dead end, it is only through God that any meaning of being can be derived.

Pursuit of Perfect Courage: Martyrdom

The meaning of courage, specifically as a moral virtue, can be derived from a differentiation of its final act, martyrdom, where the martyr gives witness to what she believes is worth dying for and why.[145] Martyrdom then becomes the highest exemplification of courage for Aquinas, following the example set by Christ. The Thomistic account looks to Christ's death as the ultimate exemplification of charity since Christ allowed himself to be crucified for those He loved. The most glaringly obvious difference between Christ and the valorous soldier in the Aristotelean account is that Christ did not engage in physical combat against His aggressors to defend the good, nor did He resist their indictments and taunts. Modeled here is strength in *spiritual* combat. In relation to Christ's ability, it then becomes evident that the Thomistic and Aristotelian accounts also differ insofar as Christ served to pursue an eternal good rather than one bound by the physical. Here, Christ's power in love is most clearly demonstrated to the virtuous agent through the courage he exhibited for love of the Father. If the agent is to both accept and respect grace infused by the Holy Spirit,

---

[145] Konyndyk De Young. "Courage as a Christian Virtue," 302.

then she can overcome any difficulty for the good. Expanding on the argument here, Christ's example serves as a model of courage by highlighting the superiority of love for the suffering or loss of life insofar as suffering may be required to pursue the good.[146] What becomes challenging in this discussion is an evaluation of the process of the agent habituating herself to accept death and endure her fate with certitude.

The martyr sees the divine good as far more important and all-encompassing than the good of earthly existence. Specifically, in the face of death, recognizing that her physical well-being is subordinate to the good of her soul, the martyr chooses, with the divine aid of grace, to endure death for a good that lies beyond this life.[147] Her fear of death is what restrains her from unduly risking the good of earthly life since the excessive suffering and agony are not goods in and of themselves. Yet when she relinquishes her life for the good, she willingly becomes an instrument of God, and since she so loves God, she will willingly accept the grace of God, which aids her in her plight.[148] The

---

[146] Konyndyk De Young, "Power made Perfect in Weakness," 170.
[147] Ibid.
[148] McKay, *The Infused and Acquired Virtues in Aquinas' Moral Philosophy*, 185.

supremacy of the infused virtues over natural virtue becomes apparent here, where her limitations and weaknesses are sustained only by the intervention of the Holy Spirit, enabling her to endure and maintain her motivation in seeking the good. The martyr surrenders herself to God and, in her act of courageous endurance, gives up her life for the good and attains the strength of the soul to withstand evil by the divine grace of the Holy Spirit.[149] In the absence of the divine grace of the Holy Spirit, she would face an immense struggle to resist temptation, with great sorrow in her sacrifice, which may no longer be intended for the sake of the good after an extended period; rather, she may eventually wish to die for her own sake to stop the emotional or physical turmoil she currently experiences.

Although martyrdom cannot be the result of habituation, the agent must still prepare her mind, which begs the question of how this may be accomplished, as death is not known to her. In this exploration of how she may prepare herself, prominent ideas emerge, including that she is motivated by her own flourishing, that she finds harmony between reason and the passions brought about by virtue, and that she acts in accord with reason for a greater end to bring about greater harmony.[150]

---

[149] Konyndyk De Young. "Courage as a Christian Virtue, " 308.

Proper preparation of the mind will allow her to remain focused on her ultimate end, and allow for her to endure her pain, and so find comfort in God. The martyr may even experience spiritual pleasure, a delight of the soul, yet she will also inevitably experience spiritual pain, a discontent in the soul due to the loss of the good of her life. Specifically, the agent experiences spiritual pleasure through the awareness of her own virtuous action, enabling her to continue in her final act.[151] Spiritual sorrow isn't problematic unless it disrupts the agent's virtuous behaviors; just as virtue demands, sorrow, too, should be appropriately directed.[152] Still, our consideration must examine martyrdom as something one undergoes rather than a purely human act.

Because the martyr can withstand the fear of death, she can also keep sight of the highest good, and in her final act, charity and courage unite her passions, where charity drives courage and allows her to face death in the defense of the good. God may infuse virtue in the agent, which further enables her ability to persevere.[153] This infused intervention enables her to

---

[150] Clark, *Perfection in Death*, 181.
[151] Konyndyk De Young, "Power made Perfect in Weakness," 173.
[152] Ibid. 176.
[153] Ibid. 168.

endure and act towards the ultimate good despite pain by conversing with God in prayer and by living a life in which she aims her actions towards the good.

CHAPTER EIGHT

COVID-19

Fear should be considered a very real and rational response to the COVID-19 pandemic for numerous reasons, including the fear of loved ones becoming ill, economic failure, and children not socializing, to name a few. The ultimate source of this fear surrounding the pandemic comes ultimately from one's own fear of death and what that may entail. The lack of socialization, even amidst the death of loved ones, compounds this fear. Schools shut down, millions lost revenue or the ability to provide for their families, and places of worship soon closed. It would appear to many that much hope was lost or broken. The ability to maintain courage during the pandemic and the ability to continue to call upon God for support would prove key to finding hope and to flourishing. This section will examine the dynamics of how God can inform courage in such a situation and how this unique relationship with God can allow one to feel more empowered during the pandemic.

Historical Context

Following that epidemics often serve as traumatizing for society, it was almost natural, especially in the Middle Ages, to respond with an attempt to find theological meaning, among other coping mechanisms. Not only would it be devastating to society to see death at every corner, but the breakdown of society and disruptions in food or supplies would further aggravate the already desperate general atmosphere.[154] During pre-modern plagues, the Church was poorly organized to handle such a crisis, with reported cases of the clergy of this time both fleeing and exploiting others, driven by motives not informed by the call to serve Christ.[155] On the other hand, great sacrifice was seen by these early

---

[154] Andrew Cunningham. "Epidemics, pandemics, and the doomsday scenario." (2008): 29
[155] Clive Pearson, "Framing a theological response to COVID-19 in the presence of the religious other." World council of Churches (2020): 851

Christians as well. For instance, the Christians faced with the Antonine plague considered the plague almost as a byproduct of a broken creation rather than of a vengeful God.[156] For instance, Cyprian, the bishop of Carthage, wrote that accepting Christ despite such hardship is a kind of martyrdom. His homilies argued not to grieve for the dead but to recognize that they are in heaven and to care for the sick.[157] Dionysius, the bishop of Alexandria, noted greatness in Christians who attended to the sick and dying, and Emperor Julian noted how the Christians would tend to the non-Christians as well.[158] With this history in the minds of Christians and their care for others, it is reasonable to assume that these individuals exhibited great courage, likely informed by the Holy Spirit, to face the danger of disease to attend to anyone in need of care.

The implications here outline an essential framework for how the Christian may respond to the COVID-19 pandemic. Fundamentally, care for others should take precedence, not only to demonstrate one's love of God but also to maintain courage. For instance, it would be far more virtuous for the agent to look after

---

[156] Ibid. 852
[157] Ibid.
[158]Clive Pearson, "Framing a theological response to COVID-19 in the presence of the religious other." World council of Churches (2020): 853

others during the pandemic by talking to them, helping them where they may struggle (think going to get groceries, for example) than it would be to carry on putting the self first. Small instances of love and care can go to great lengths to help others in their struggles with the pandemic, and by practicing care for others, we may deepen our love for God. Although it would be courageous to continue to work, whether at a factory, grocery store, or hospital, small instances of courage (i.e., risks of COVID) to help others still make a significant difference to the virtuous agent and the individual they help.

COVID-19 and Virtue

At the height of the pandemic, many were left alone and unable to see loved ones due to fear of either getting the virus themselves or passing it along. In a recent study, 66 percent of people considered COVID to be a high risk for their children, 53 percent considered COVID a high risk for their parents, and 70 percent considered COVID a high risk for their friends.[159] In addition to fears about loved ones becoming ill, 41 percent of participants identified economic issues as

---

[159] Morning Consult Poll, see bibliography.

their priority concern.[160] From this, we can draw a general picture of how Americans felt during the pandemic, that Americans were concerned about the welfare of their families and friends, as can be seen in data supporting their concern if they were to get ill. In addition, Americans were worried about the state of their economy, which was negatively impacted during the course of the pandemic. The general state of fear in the country can be characterized by a feeling of dreadful anxiety about the uncertainty of the pandemic and its potential aftermath. In the case of COVID-19, what difference, if any, would virtue make for those most afflicted?

Let us first recall that virtue enables us to find the mean between two extremes to better pursue the good. Fowers et al. identify three key challenges posed by the pandemic and how virtue can allow for flourishing when it doesn't seem possible.[161] The first challenge of the pandemic is that of risk, in which we face the risk of a virus, as well as the possibility of systematic violence against marginalized groups.[162] This definition of risk during the pandemic allows for a

---

[160] Ibid.
[161] Fowers et al, "Courage, Justice, and Practical Wisdom as Key Virtues in the Era of COVID-19," 2.
[162] Ibid.

visualization of the driving forces that make us feel at risk. For marginalized groups, this risk is intensified because of systematic injustices, including equitable healthcare. With the lack of socialization due to the pandemic, the ability to share these burdens with others becomes more difficult, and the ability to arrive at solutions incorporating the community's input becomes near impossible. Risk, therefore, drives a sense of fear in the community of the virus, which is enhanced for marginalized groups. It disables community-wide decision-making, and discussion aimed at healthy solutions for the community. Injustice is the second key challenge posed by the pandemic and can be characterized by unequal treatment. Fowers et al. call attention to how blue-collar workers received less than acceptable recognition during the pandemic for their contributions to the effort against the virus.[163] Part of this unequal treatment not only fails to recognize the efforts of these workers but also the unnecessary risks they take. A physician or nurse should be able to accept some of the risks posed by the pandemic compared to those cleaning the isolation units or the receptionists at doctors' offices, for example. Finally, the third major challenge of the pandemic is its sheer complexity.

---

[163] Ibid.

Complexity refers to the vast encompassing spectrum of issues the pandemic has caused, including how governments handle COVID-related challenges and policies, as well as how schools educate their students.[164] In short, the pandemic has brought injustices, risks, and vast complexities to the surface, to which people are unable to respond appropriately without virtue. Virtue enables collective effort in a meaningful way, seeking change and progress aimed at the good.

One of the priorities of COVID policies was to keep children from contracting the virus and spreading it to those at home who may have compromised immune systems. UNICEF published data that reported on how children globally were affected by COVID, which raised points not typically called into discussion. The initial solution to learning during the pandemic was online learning. However, UNICEF reports that at least 463 million children were unable to access remote learning.[165] In addition, the published data indicated that upwards of 370 million missed school meals, and of the reported 132 million that lacked substantial food in 2020, 44 million of these were children.[166] In addition,

---

[164] Ibid. 3.
[165] "COVID-19 and Children," UNICEF, nd.
[166] Ibid.

the Pew Research Center published data reporting that 61 percent of American parents viewed COVID's impact on education as very or somewhat negative, and 48 percent said their children's emotional well-being was impacted very or somewhat negatively.[167] The fundamental question regarding COVID learning is how to strike a proper balance between in-person education and public safety. Both of these concerns are valid, the concern for public safety on the one hand and the concern for quality education on the other. I find that the solution to this problem is far less clear than the dilemma of whether one should get vaccinated since both sides seem to have equally valuable goods in mind and make equally strong cases for prioritizing the good, they deem to be primary.

Religion in the Context of COVID-19

During a pandemic, it is natural to feel scared, fearful, hopeless, and lonely all at once. In such a situation, two divergent options emerge: one in which God is the governing reality of the universe and the other where we do not acknowledge Him. However,

---

[167] Braga, Dana & Parker, Kim, "Most K-12 parents say first year of pandemic had a negative effect on their children's education," Oct, 2022.

one of the fundamental issues during the pandemic was limited access to places of worship, which in turn made the pandemic that much more difficult. We can still confide in God without being in a church and find comfort in His word. For Catholics, some of the most powerful words in the Church can be found in the Nicene Creed, the "Hail Mary," and the "Our Father." The Nicene Creed speaks of the forgiveness God has for us, our call to be resurrected with Him, and our eternal life with Him. This creed can help one remember what is important, that loving others and God cannot and will not be shaped by our present fear of the virus, for He will always be with us and is always ready to have us confide our fears in Him. Those who do not believe in God can only confide their fears in other people. Regardless, while people may or may not love us, God will always love us as He promised. It takes much courage from the atheist to believe in God without the sort of conclusive evidence they may desire; it requires acting despite the lack of complete certainty and control, just as the call to love during the pandemic requires courage, insofar as one acts in the face of present dangers and fears. The act of faith on the part of the atheist requires courage to the extent that it ventures an answer to the question of ultimate meaning and so serves as a lens for understanding the human condition and death, the greatest fear. In short, the courage required by the atheist to take part in faith is great in magnitude because this provides meaning and depth to life.

But does religious faith really help individuals cope with COVID or with the rapidly changing world that accompanied its onslaught? If so, how and why? Ken-En Gan et al. discuss how religious social support better facilitates individuals' mental well-being during the pandemic. Before the study, they acknowledged a general correlation between religion and well-being, where religion provides "integrated reasoning structures,[168] namely the ability for the individual to find hope as well as a more positive mindset during arduous times.[169] They noted that this ability was found largely in individuals with support systems, including religious groups, family, and friends, while discussing the contrary, where individuals with low social support correlated with a higher likelihood of depression and other psychological distress.[170] In short, individuals with

---

[168] Samuel Ken-En Gal et. Al, "Religiosity, theism, perceived social support, resilience, and well-being of University undergraduate students in Singapore during the COVID-19 pandemic." International Journal of environmental research and public health, no 20 (2023): 1.
[169] Ibid. 2.

a strong support network were less likely to suffer distress than those without strong social support. This makes sense, yet the lack of social contact during the pandemic certainly proved difficult for individuals to socialize and maintain that strong support network needed. In the instance of organized religious groups, namely Catholic, the lack of a physical presence in the Mass or even for individuals who could not receive the sacraments during the pandemic would prove difficult since these help provide a sense of unity and belonging with others.

Courage and COVID

If courage is the virtue that enables rational decision-making in the face of challenge, then it should be the virtue driving decision-making during the pandemic. Courage allows for one to take a risk while putting fear aside in order to pursue the good. Again, this exemplification of courage must be met with a proper balance of confidence and fear. It should be clear that frontline workers exemplify courage because they take calculated risks for the betterment of their

170 Ibid.

community. The component of courage that deals with fear should not be in excess, as this would force one to feel the need to be completely isolated from the outside world. On the other hand, a lack of fear would make one reckless and could consequently spread the virus knowingly or unknowingly. Therefore, the appropriate amount of courage will enable flourishing during the pandemic.

As the key virtue pertaining to risk-taking for the good, one must consider how courage is exhibited in the average person and how such a person contributes to the good of the community. For example, society tended to deem staying indoors and away from others courageous during the pandemic. Upon closer inspection, however, we must identify the proper balance between confidence and fear for a behavior to be considered courageous. One could argue that the risk could be from social isolation, yet the moderation of risk is hard to define. One could mitigate risk by staying away from others, which could be deemed courageous to some extent. In my opinion, a higher exemplification of courage can be seen in the average person's decision-making process in vaccination or how a teacher strives to teach and engage students despite the challenges present.

For the average family, I would argue that the case for the education of children demands the most courage to pursue the greatest good. As mentioned above, there is no perfect solution; on one end of the spectrum, children could become infected with COVID and readily transmit the virus at home, and at the other end, children lack the education they deserve. The act of pursuing the best outcome for children demands courage since there are risks to both possible solutions, meaning that no matter which course one takes, one's actions will require courage. Following this, recognizing the truest good must be evaluated to guide the individual and her decision-making here; this typical exemplification of courage should be regarded as the courage that aims to find the proper balance of risk with respect to the dangers on both sides of the problem. Yet even in this case, the courage exemplified by believers and nonbelievers are categorically different since the theistic individual aims all her actions towards God and what or whom the atheistic individual aims at may fluctuate from situation to situation or lack altogether. In other words, the aims of the theistic individual are clear since they are aimed at God, and the subordinate actions which call for courage are made clear by this distinction.

In contrast, the atheistic individual may not have a clear aim or priority. She may rather act with courage for a more immediate and a good which is not as perfect as those found in God. This is not to say that atheists lack a hierarchy of goods, as presented in Aristotelean thought, yet they often fail to recognize the source or highest form of goods in God. In addition to this discussion on masks, vaccinations, and education during COVID, it should be recognized that there are more mundane examples of courage exemplified by the average layperson. Going to the supermarket at the beginning of the pandemic clearly called for some sort of courage, given the risk and fear that came along with the unknowns about COVID. Going to the doctor's office or visiting loved ones demanded courage, as did going to work to keep the economy moving, serving in pivotal roles in healthcare, driving a truck to deliver vital equipment, vaccines, or food, answering the phones in the hospital, and ensuring a clean environment in the hospital, to name a few.

Vaccines

For vaccination to be virtuous, one must first carefully reflect upon and understand the risks and benefits involved, which implies seeking out a greater understanding of vaccinations in some way, even if this includes being patient with trials and published data. In some cases, this decision may be easier; for example, those working with and around those who are sick may benefit more from vaccination than those who don't since the risk of contracting COVID would be higher in hospitals and clinics. Those who do not work in medical environments may consider the benefit of reducing the severity of infection, but they may also deem that benefit as not worth the risk if the individual has medical conditions that place them at higher risk for vaccine complications.

Receiving a vaccine can be an act of courage, but only if it is both prudent and just to do so, given the relative risks and benefits involved. Prudence elicits and regulates the other virtues, while justice seeks the common good of the community through "an equitable distribution [of] burdens and benefits."[171] The virtue of courage calls for a proper balancing of fear, which is

---

[171] Fowers et al, "Courage, Justice, and Practical Wisdom as Key Virtues in the Era of COVID-19," 6.

beneficial to the individual to make informed decisions. This would mean that deciding to get vaccinated first requires the exercise of prudence. Prudence allows one to see the benefits and costs of each course of action. The burden of receiving the vaccination could include a lack of trust in the medical system or authorities or a sense of guilt regarding the fetal cell lines used to research such vaccines. One who deems vaccination immoral in cases where fetal cells are used to develop the vaccine would exemplify courage by facing the dangers of being unvaccinated for the sake of what they regard as a higher good, namely just action with respect to unborn human life. The benefits to the individual and the community include fewer symptoms if an individual is infected with COVID, a lower chance of facing medical complications if symptoms are severe, and a decreased likelihood of spreading the virus.[172] The risks of receiving the vaccine could include side effects and, in some cases, severe medical conditions such as myocarditis.[173]

What I find key here is that both getting vaccinated and abstaining from vaccination involve

---

[172] David Eyre et. Al. "Effect of Covid-19 Vaccination on Transmission of Alpha and Delta Variants." New England Journal of Medicine (2022).

[173] Joseph Fraiman et. Al. "Serious adverse events of special interest following mRNA COVID-19 vaccination in randomized trials in adults." Vaccine no. 40 (2022): 5798-5805.

risks. What makes facing the risks in either case an act of courage is an individual's prudent evaluation of the potential costs and benefits involved, given the circumstances of their situation. For instance, it would be more courageous for someone especially vulnerable to the virus or who lives with someone more vulnerable to accept the risks of vaccination, while it would also be courageous for someone vulnerable to the side effects of the vaccine to forego it and accept the risks of contracting the virus. Thus, if the individual's intent is sound and in accord with reason, either course of action could be courageous. It is the intent of the individual with respect to their community or family that determines whether or not vaccination is courageous. One may be exposed to people who either push strongly for vaccinations for all or adamantly oppose them for all. Individuals could even risk forms of backlash from said people, including discrimination or harassment. Therefore, I argue that one should deliberate the effects of vaccination for oneself and the community in light of their own circumstances and then take action with this deliberation in mind, given the particular goods at stake in their particular situation. If an individual thinks clearly about the implications of the vaccination for themselves and the community at large, and properly weighs the risks involved, then their decision to face the dangers required to pursue the greatest good at stake will result in a courageous act. The key issue that remains is the state of the conscience, in which a good conscience informed by a good will always trump the tendency to act against one's deepest convictions about the highest good for the sake of avoiding proximate difficulties or enjoying lower goods. Here, the good conscience allows the individual to make a clear and effective judgment while minimizing the negative downsides of her decisions or actions, whereas the bad conscience may lack this entirely. Specifically, this minimization here will regulate fear with respect to the pursued goods and maintain a proper proportion between the present dangers and her ultimate aims. It is obvious then that the good conscience follows the patterns of virtue, proving virtue's role in the COVID-19 pandemic, including vaccinations. It should be noted the individual conscience very well may be silenced or disregarded, even if it is in the name of public safety. The larger point here is to value the individual and her conscience to guide her actions since suppressing one's conscience to conformity is an active form of oppression and violates the nature of human dignity.[174]

Masks and the Theology of the Face

The exemplification of courage during COVID, as in any other circumstance, is at its highest form when risk is greatest. The risk of vaccination lies mainly within an individual domain, insofar as the greatest risk to receiving the vaccine would be personal freedom, which is overridden by some governing entity—an employer, school, etc.—or a health-related concern. In the case of schooling, the risks parents and schools must balance involve how much they are willing to risk infection for the sake of in-person learning. In the case of masks, as with vaccinations, the biggest risk to the individual comes down to individual freedom to choose whether the benefits of masking outweigh the drawbacks. For example, Elisheva Rosner presents many of the adverse drawbacks of prolonged mask-wearing, namely in healthcare professionals.[175] In this discussion, it was

---

[174] I would like to emphasize that I take no position here regarding vaccination. I am not a medical professional, and I only share my opinions. The key point I make here is to think virtuously; for many it is virtuous to receive a vaccine, and for others it may not be. While maintaining the good of the public should be of a primary concern, it need not be the only point of concern. As I mentioned, one may be hesitant to receive the vaccine due to ethical or moral dilemmas they may have. Regardless, as Christians, we are called to love others despite differences in opinion. Respect goes a long way, and we as followers of Christ are upheld to a high standard to love others as Christ so did.

confirmed that there was an increase in physiological and psychological burdens in the participants of the study; specifically, there was an increase in carbon dioxide, which causes impaired cognition and headaches, as well as increases in acne on the face, and in some cases contact dermatitis from sensitivity to the masks, or other PPE used.[176] The point here is not to dissuade anyone from wearing masks, especially considering that Mello et al. confirmed that the median load of viral RNA for individuals wearing no masks was significantly greater than for those who masked, namely a difference of an extra thousand copies of viral RNA in individuals without masks.[177] As will be discussed, the courage demanded in this situation requires that the individual deliberate on what is best for herself and her community and then act upon that deliberation. The intervention of the Grace from the Holy Spirit better enables her to make such deliberations, while infused courage better enables her to act after her whole and complete deliberation.

---

[175] Elishiva Rosner, "Adverse effects of prolongs mask use among healthcare professionals during COVID-19." *Journal of Infectious Diseases and Epidemiology,* no. 6 (2020): 130.
[176] Ibid.
[177] Mello et. Al, "Effectiveness of face masks in blocking the transmission of SARS-CoV2: A preliminary evaluation of masks used by SARS-CoV-2-infected individuals." *PLOS ONE,* no. 2 (2022).

One point to consider when discussing masks is the theological importance of the face. The face represents a unique representation of the person and, in biblical texts, often signifies the importance of the speaker. Likewise, hiding the face in biblical scripture signifies humanity's sinful self-distortion after the fall. Regularly wearing a mask in public thus carries with it important theological-symbolic meaning.[178] Following this point, an individual's face represents who they are; it is where we look when we speak and express emotion. In social terms, when one hides their face, they obstruct their ability to connect with others through the sight of one. This is not to say the face is the only thing that makes one unique, but it is one of the central parts of what makes a person unique. In the Bible, God revealing his face is a great sign of love, whereas the hiding of His face represents displeasure.[179] To Catholics and other Christians, the image of Christ's face on the Shroud of Turin epitomizes the significance of the face for the kind of personal connection to God made possible through holy images. This image of Christ's face demonstrates the suffering and sacrifice of

---

[178] Joshua Farris, "A theology of faces: notes on the costs of masking." Mere Orthodoxy (2020).
[179] Ibid.

Christ's body, allowing for another means of interaction with Christ; by seeing His Holy face.

Physicians, Healthcare Workers, and COVID

First responders and medical professionals were called to a higher order of courage than other individuals and families. This call to service went above and beyond the typical call of duty, especially when COVID first became a global threat with all its unknowns. The courage exemplified here could even be thought imprudent, especially if those working close with COVID patients became infected themselves and then spread the virus to more vulnerable family members. The mention of prudence here is to not conjure the idea that frontline workers were irrational or didn't consider their duties and safety in accord with practical reason. What I am suggesting is that it could be argued that some could view working closely with the infected as imprudent and, therefore, reckless. Many may not have had much choice as to whether or not they wanted to risk exposure to a relatively unknown threat and potentially get family members sick, yet they, too, are called to courage. In this specific instance, I argue that for those frontline workers and medical professionals who did not want to risk their own safety but worked regardless, courage involved facing risk for the sake of preserving the greater good of their livelihoods and careers. To be clearer on this point, the end must be good insofar as they aim to promote the flourishing of the community at large. The nature of the individual's aims towards the good is what demands attention, this however becomes a difficult point since those acting may perceive their actions to be normative for the rest of the world, whereas only the facts of the situation can dictate whether or not their actions were courageous. Specifically, here, the good must be exemplified by the bettering of the human race or by promoting the flourishing of others, as this represents the highest good ordered by God, in which we love God by serving others. The prudence exemplified in this scenario may be of a different form than those who willingly wanted to work and serve those who were infected. Say, for example, a frontline worker does not find it justifiable to work and potentially get their family members infected but continues to work in order to provide for their family. The prudence exemplified here follows a clear logic in which their aim is to accept that health risk to support their families, whereas those less reluctant to work in a high-risk environment exemplified prudence by simply wanting to preserve the life and well-being of others. Both cases involve individuals taking risks beyond their typical work duties, calling for the courage to inform their decision to work to help the sick, provide for their families, or both.

Besides COVID, courage empowered by the Holy Spirit can guide and inform physicians in their actions by ordering them to pursue the highest good. Yet we should now discuss how theism may aid the individual and how this is possible. Dr. Jose Florez, a Catholic physician at Massachusetts General Hospital in Boston, finds that his role as a physician allows him to follow and imitate Christ by aiding the vulnerable and their healing.[180] In addition, he finds that prayer allows him to connect with his patients in ways that are meaningful and comforting to them.[181] Why might prayer and an intimate relationship with the Holy Spirit better aid physicians and healthcare workers in finding comfort in themselves and empathizing with their patients? First, God grounds us insofar as we come to know and recognize in Him all that is good, namely

---

[180] A place for faith: Doctors bring spirituality to work, AAMC.
[181] Ibid.

love. This chief principle then allows the physician to care for the patient on an intimate level as a means of following Christ. The physician is then better able to empathize and care for the weak and vulnerable. Next, God provides a source of comfort for the patients themselves, for healthcare workers, and the families of both. This is of vital importance since the support of the Divine allows these individuals to find peace and solidarity, especially during crises or suffering. The way in which one may do this includes prayer but isn't limited to prayer alone. As a follower of Christ, the physician or nurse may find comfort in knowing they have sacrificed something for their patients, which may include knowing they have given their full effort, body, and mind, to better serve their patients. In this way, the mind and heart of the individual can be informed by the Holy Spirit to remain fixated upon love for the patient, which will better guide them to treating the patient, as well as empathizing and remaining compassionate with them. For the patients, comfort in the Divine may be found through prayer as well so as to reflect on the Divine Good and the love in this world and the many gifts and treasures we may have. They may also find comfort in God by sharing their experiences and engaging in a meaningful reflection on life. As for families, the Divine intervention of the Holy Spirit brings comfort to them by assuring them that their loved ones have done their best to attend to their patients or, in the case of the patients' families, that they have done their best to care for the soul of their loved ones in order to bring peace to them. In a larger sense, the Church may act as a support network for families of healthcare workers and the sick, allowing love to be the principal force driving the good, in addition to the celebration of the Holy Eucharist.

Virtue ethics provides the most adequate account of how the physician can best treat the patient and remain fixated upon the highest good. To begin, decisions in healthcare should be made with due respect and compassion and not devoid of emotion since due regard for all the dimensions of human action better enables the physician to act for the good of their patients.[182] Emotion plays an integral role in ensuring decisions in medicine are treated with careful consideration and can better illuminate perceptions of the case, which can better allow for a more holistic approach.[183] If emotion were to be devoid in this

[182] P Gardiner, "A virtue ethics approach to moral dilemmas in medicine." Journal of Medical Ethics, no. 5 (2003): 297.
[183] Ibid. 298.

process, the physician would lack the ability to empathize with the patient and could overlook this holistic approach, which allows the physician to remain fully human and feel for the patient. The compassionate physician also considers the patient's welfare and needs, especially when vulnerable, and recognizes how their treatments or plans may affect the patient and their family. Incorporating all of these elements into the physician's treatment for the patient ensures that decisions are ethically guided and allows for a connection between provider and patient, as well as a better ability to empathize. However, it is still beneficial for the physician to receive Divine support as this most reliably grounds her motivations in love and so maintains her vision of the patient, along with all the aspects of her situation that would inform proper judgment and authentic care.

The larger point to be made, specifically in the context of the Thomistic arguments for meaning and virtue presented here, is that there is an array of fears and issues which the COVID-19 pandemic tends to throw at society. These issues include whether or not one should receive a vaccine or wear masks, whether and when children should return to school, and what should be done about depression and other mental health issues aggravated by isolation, just to name a few. The virtuous individual has the ability, acquired through habituation, to make informed decisions ordered for the good. Now, this ability serves the agent by allowing her to have the habituated tendency to think and make decisions rationally and thoughtfully, with their aims focused upon the good. Such decisions become problematic when there is no habituation in play, or when the circumstances offer too many unknowns, or too many complicated details and factors for practical reason alone to consider. In this scenario, the agent with the gift of infused virtue of courage can rely upon the Divine Intervention of the Holy Spirit to guide her towards the ultimate good of friendship with God, most fundamentally by loving others. What makes infused courage particularly advantageous to the individual struggling amidst the pandemic can be seen in numerous ways: (1) the individual has Divine assistance in making decisions and acting with courage in the face of the pandemic, especially since several challenges pertaining to the COVID-19 pandemic are ones which we as a society have not encountered in our lifetimes; (2) the emotional burdens of the pandemic can be supported and cared for by the love of God, especially since increased isolation and stressors are so very new during COVID; and (3) infused courage and Divine assistance enable us to remain fixed upon loving others during this unprecedented time. Therefore, it only makes sense then that Divine assistance, aiding the individual with the gift of infused courage, enables her to flourish and withstand the pressures and challenges of the pandemic more so than natural courage alone.

CONCLUSION

The structure of this discussion first emphasized God as source for the objective good, made evident with comparison to the Nietzschean account of reality and morality in which Nietzsche argues the will to power is the biological instinct of humans, whereas the Christian account defines the true objective good by a call to the good through love. Following this, it was demonstrated that despite the faults of human reason and their inability to prove God, Pascal demonstrates that we are called to God by the will and our innate desire for happiness, in which this condition of happiness is never perfectly satisfied without God. Since God is the objective good, where this relationship is based upon one's ability and/or desire to love others, the remainder of the discussion serves to emphasize how one may achieve this relationship with God through the virtue of charity.

The larger point of this discussion served to highlight how courage enables the virtuous agent to flourish during pandemics and how this explication may be informed. Although there is little structural difference between the acquired and infused virtues, the solidarity found in God enables the agent to maintain composure and rely upon God as a fundamental support, aiding her in the pursuit of the good. Uncertainty during the COVID-19 pandemic has led many to question their faith or the existence of God, let alone the possibility of flourishing. This discussion highlights how infused virtue reinforces courage and other acts of moral integrity that prioritize what is right for oneself and one's family. Primarily, the gift of infused courage enables one to make sound judgments and pursue the good despite dangers, embodying the teachings of Christ. When one recognizes this ability to find love in God, and by virtue of courage, she may come to flourish during the COVID-19 pandemic. This divine assistance assures the individual peace and love and propels her towards the good and the ability to flourish, specifically in regard to the COVID-19 pandemic, courage is the virtue that enables the individual to rationally think and make decisions, and when this is informed by the Holy Spirit rather than habituation, which is problematic since many of the challenges of the pandemic may be new for many, then courage can drive her ability to thrive.

The takeaway here should remain that the demands of COVID-19, no matter how new or challenging, can be responded to with courage. Facing this challenge with courage will enable the individual to (1) make morally correct decisions for herself and her family, whether this includes issues of masking, vaccinations, education for children, parents, or adults working, to name a few; (2) the gift of infused courage will enable her to maintain a relationship with God and by doing this enables her to be reminded of the love of God, and she may better love her community to enable them to flourish as well; and (3) infused courage will enable her to support herself and her community, to provide value or compassion to others. These instances of courage are neither novel nor new; rather, these instances are simply forgotten when the world is comfortable, safe, and healthy. The individuals of past pandemics who exhibited great courage also serve as great exemplars for Catholics today during the COVID-19 pandemic. Yet, when comfortable, we may forget how courage is demanded in such circumstances.

Regarding a theistic perspective, one may ask if and when the world is comfortable, God is forgotten, and when the world is in shambles, God is here to be the scapegoat of our suffering. God can never be forgotten as long as there is good and love, and daily instances of love for others clearly demonstrate that the natural inclinations of the will are to love always. When the world is suffering, though many become frightened, and rightfully so, we remain and always will be a broken creation since the original justice in Eden. In other words, we are to feel pain, we are to suffer, and we are to die, none of which was a part of God's plan. To suffer is to live in reality, and one may argue that small instances of suffering aid the individual in recognizing the good and how love truly compels her to do good, love, and find God. We all must suffer, and to do so courageously as Christ did, as the martyrs have done, and many will continue to do, we must find the good in God and love others so that we may too be granted the gifts of the Holy Spirit including infused courage, and love, persevere, and carry on when hope may run low.

Bibliography

"A place for faith: Doctors bring spirituality to work,"
    AAMC. Accessed April 1, 2023.
    https://www.aamc.org/news-insights/place-
    faith-doctors-bring-spirituality-work

"More Americans Than People in Other Advanced
    Economies Say COVID-19 Has Strengthened
    Religious Faith," Pew Research. (2021).
    https://www.pewresearch.org/religion/2021/0
    1/27/more-americans-than-people-in-other-
    advanced-economies-say-covid-19-has-
    strengthened-religious-faith/

Armitage, Duane. *Heidegger and the Death of God: Between
    Plato and Nietzsche.* Cham: Springer International
    Publishing, 2017.

Armitage, Duane. *Philosophy's Violent Sacred; Heidegger and
    Nietzsche through Mimetic Theory.* Studies in

Violence, Mimesis, and Culture. East Lansing: Michigan State University, 2021.

Benamon, Patricia. "Keeping the Faith: A Healthcare Workers Story of Burnout." *BioLogos* November 2022.

Boyle, Patrick. "A place for faith: Doctors bring spirituality to work." *AAMC.* (2022).

Braga, Dana & Parker, Kim, "Most K-12 parents say first year of pandemic had a negative effect on their children's education," *Pew Research Center,* October, 2022.

Catholic Church. "Catechism of the Catholic Church." 2nd ed. Huntingdon, PA: Our Sunday Visitor, 2000.

Clark, Patrick. "Is Martyrdom Virtuous? An Occasion for Rethinking the Relation of Christ and Virtue in Aquinas." *Journal of the Society of Christian Ethics* 30, no. 1 (2010): 141-159.

Clark, Patrick. *Perfection in Death.* United States: The Catholic University of America Press, 2015.

Cottingham, John. *Why Believe?.* London: Continuum, 2009.

Darnell, Fowers, and Kristjánsson. "A Multifunction Approach to Assessing Aristotelian Phronesis

(Practical Wisdom)." *Personality and Individual Differences 196*, (October 2022): 1-10.

Eyre, David et. Al. "Effect of Covid-19 Vaccination on Transmission of Alpha and Delta Variants." *New England Journal of Medicine* (2022).

Farris, Joshua, "A theology of faces: Notes on the costs of masking." Mere Orthodoxy (2020).

Fowers, Novak, Calder, and Sommer. "Courage, Justice, and Practical Wisdom as Key Virtues in the Era of COVID-19." *Frontiers in Psychology 12* (March 2021): 1-11.

Fraiman, J. et. Al. "Serious adverse events of special interest following mRNA COVID-19 vaccination in randomized trials in adults." *Vaccine* no. 40 (2022): 5798-5805.

Goff, Philip. "Our Improbable Existence Is No Evidence for a Multiverse," *Scientific American.* (2021).

Greach, Peter. *The Virtues.* Cambridge University Press, 1977.

Ken-En Gal, S. et al., "Religiosity, theism, perceived social support, resilience, and well-being of University undergraduate students in Singapore during the COVID-19 pandemic." *International*

Journal of environmental research and public health, no. 20 (2023).

Khubchandani, Jagdish et. Al. "Post-lockdown depression and anxiety in the USA during the COVID-19 pandemic," *Journal of Public Health,* (2021).

Konyndyk DeYoung, Rebecca. "Courage as a Christian Virtue," *Journal of Spiritual Formation and Soul Care* 6, no. 2 (2013): 301-312.

Konyndyk DeYoung, Rebecca. "Power Made Perfect in Weakness: Aquinas's Transformation of the Virtue of Courage," *Medieval Philosophy and Theology* 11, no. 2 (2003): 147-180.

Levering, Matthew. *Proofs of God.* Grand Rapids: Baker Academic, 2016.

MacIntyre, Alasdair. "The Nature of the Virtues." The Hastings Center, 1981.

McKay, Angela. "The Infused and Acquired Virtues in Aquinas' Moral Philosophy," PhD diss., (University of Notre Dame, 2004).

Mello, VM. et. Al, "Effectiveness of face masks in blocking the transmission of SARS-CoV2: A preliminary evaluation of masks used by SARS-CoV-2-infected individuals." P*LOS ONE*, no. 2 (2022).

Morning Consult + New York Times. National
       Tracking Poll #200821. August 2020.

Otswald, Martin, and Aristotle. *Nicomachean Ethics*. New
       Jersey: Prentice Hall, 1962.

P. Gardiner, "A virtue ethics approach to moral
       dilemmas in medicine." *Journal of Medical Ethics*,
       no 5 (2003): 297-302.

Pearson, Clive, "Framing a theological response to
       COVID-19 in the presence of the religious
       other." *World Council of Churches* (2020): 849-860

Pieper, Josef. *The Four Cardinal Virtues: Prudence, Justice,*
       Fortitude, Temperance. Twentieth Century
       Religious Thought, Volume I: Christianity.
       Notre Dame, IN: University of Notre Dame
       Press, 2010.

Qiaoying, Lu. "Aquinas's Transformation of the Virtue
       of Courage." *Frontiers of Philosophy in China* 8, no
       3 (2013): 471-484.

Rigoli, Francesco. "The Link Between COVID-19,
       Anxiety, and Religious Beliefs in the United
       States and the United Kingdom," *Journal of*
       Religion and Health 60, no. 4 (2021): 2196-2208.

Rosner, Elissheva. "Adverse effects of prolonged mask
       use among healthcare professionals during

COVID-19." *Journal of Infectious Diseases and Epidemiology,* no 6 (2020).

"COVID-19 and Children," UNICEF. Accessed December 1, 2022. https://data.unicef.org/covid-19-and-children/

www.ingramcontent.com/pod-product-compliance
Lightning Source LLC
Chambersburg PA
CBHW051728040426
42447CB00008B/1029